How to Know You'll Live Forever!

HOW TO KNOW YOU'LL LIVE FOREVER!

Richard Dugan

BETHANY HOUSE PUBLISHERS
MINNEAPOLIS, MINNESOTA 55438
A Division of Bethany Fellowship, Inc.

Scripture quotations are from the King James Version of the Bible.
Those indicated (NASB) are from the New American Standard Bible. Copyright © The Lockman Foundation, 1971. Used by permission.

Formerly published under the title *How to Know You Are Born Again*

This edition has been revised.

Library of Congress Catalog Card Number 84–70727
ISBN 0–87123–312–6
Copyright © 1984
Richard Dugan
All Rights Reserved

Published by Bethany House Publishers
A Division of Bethany Fellowship, Inc.
6820 Auto Club Road, Minneapolis, Minnesota 55438

Printed in the United States of America

DEDICATION

To my wife, Priscilla, and our five wonderful children for whom my ultimate concern is that they experience and walk in the truth contained in this book.

Preface

From Day One men have pondered the secrets of longevity. How to live longer, better, and happier has monopolized the minds of men everywhere.

The secret was lost on that dark day when Adam and Eve were thrust from the Garden by an angel with flaming sword. Behind and ever closed to them was the Tree of Life and with it the secret of living forever. In its place was left the haunting legacy of aging and death.

The pharaohs of Egypt certainly wanted to live forever. When they discovered they could not, they built pyramids to immortalize their deeds and preserve their corpses for thousands of years. But they scarcely found what Adam lost.

In 1513 Spanish explorer Ponce de Leon responded to Indian lore concerning the existence of a "fountain of youth" and proceeded to comb both the island of Bimini and the state of Florida, sipping from every spring he encountered.

Actually, the Indians were only repeating a legend they had heard from white men who were referring to the Water of Life found in the Garden of Eden, which Europeans presumed to be in the Far East.

Eight years later Juan Ponce de Leon died in Cuba, hardly coming close to what Adam lost.

The search continued, this time in mid-eighteenth-century England. On a quiet back street, Sunday after Sunday, the deacons sat through many a sermon, listening irritably to the minister's seemingly monotonous repetition of Jesus' words to Nicodemus: "Ye must be born again." The parson did speak with conviction, it was true, but enough was enough! How much longer must the pious endure?

Testily the deacons approached him. "Why do you continue to preach, 'You must be born again'?"

John Wesley, for it was he, answered simply: "Because you must be born again!"

John Wesley himself had experienced the miracle of being born again in a little Moravian chapel on Aldersgate Street, London, where he had taken refuge for his exhausted soul. On his return from Georgia, the American colony, as a missionary to the Indians, he was devastated by his failure as a missionary.

Concentrating on the words as the leader read Luther's introduction to the book of Romans, he came into a spiritual rebirth that was to transform the religious life in England and, eventually, in America.

As the words of Luther reached him, Wesley was moved to stand and abruptly express the miracle he was undergoing. He said: "Brethren, just now my heart is strangely warmed. I feel that I do trust Christ, and Christ alone, for my salvation."

It was in that moment John Wesley was born again. Thirteen years of futile labor had made him a prime candidate for the spiritual link with divine power that accompanies the new birth. And it was from the freshness of his "strangely warmed" heart that the series of sermons issued which so vexed the spiritually dead in his congregation.

Trekking by horseback an average of sixty or seventy miles a day and tirelessly writing every night, he spread this transforming message across the British Isles until he died at the age of eighty-eight.

Wesley had discovered the fountain of eternal youth, and though his body faltered and expired, his spirit soared into fulfillment of Jesus' words to Martha: "He that believeth in me, though he were dead, yet shall he live; and whosoever liveth and believeth in me *shall never die*." Wesley found what Adam lost. He discovered how to live forever.

The golden gateway to "forever living" is opened by the New Birth. The following chapters are dedicated to that subject. The New Birth—"What is it?" "Who needs it?" "How does it happen?" and most of all, "How can I know it has happened to me?"—these questions will be answered in that order on the pages to follow; this little book will help you to know that you are going to live forever.

Please understand we are speaking of more than mere longevity. Tell a despondent man he will live forever, and you have not been to him a bearer of good news. The best such a state of mind can hope for is oblivion or "nirvana," a state of nothingness, and often that hope is pursued by suicide. No, we are speaking of a *quality* of life that begins right here on earth and goes on into eternity.

We are saying that the new birth will introduce us to the quality of life that is characterized by joy, hope, peace, con-

tentment, and a sense of purpose and fulfillment, a place where boredom is forever
banished. We are presenting a quality of
life, here and now, that gives meaning and
worth to living *even if there were no
heaven or hell*.

Since the Bible clearly teaches there *is*
the prospect of one or the other for every
person, this book, HOW TO KNOW
YOU'LL LIVE FOREVER, shows you how to
choose life eternal with God.

Contents

Chapter 1

The New Birth: What Is It?

A few years ago I found myself coaching wrestling in a small high school in eastern South Dakota. With just a few boys, some mighty poor equipment and very little time, I set about to prepare the team for their first meet. I'd had enough experience to be scornful of the coach who could not control himself during a contest. So, the day of the meet found me sitting quietly on the visitors' bench with clipboard (all coaches carry clipboards) in one hand and tape recorder in the other.

As the meet proceeded, two negatives quickly surfaced. The first was the officiating—it was lousy. Once a wrestler myself, and later an official, I was sure I knew everything. Soon I was on my feet shouting corrections at the bungling referee. It was following the referee's plainly implied "sit down-shut up" that the second negative became clear. Those boys, *my* boys, had an uncanny talent for making the right moves at the wrong time and the wrong moves at the right time.

In short, they beat themselves. The season produced one fellow who was the most innovative of all—he found a new way to get pinned in every match.

How did the coach feel about all of this? Frustrated, truly frustrated.

If only there was a way that I could get inside of those kids' uniforms—better yet, inside their skins and into their minds. If only I could make them the instant beneficiary of my knowledge of wrestling! In the league we competed in they would have been transformed from losers to winners.

Parents feel the same way. Note the expression on mother's face as Johnny struggles to remember his verse in the Christmas program. If only she could make him the instant beneficiary of her knowledge of the poem, she could save him (and herself) from failure and embarrassment.

Senior citizens surely must suffer as

they see a new generation blunder along, without the guidance their wisdom could provide.

Now if coaches, parents and senior citizens suffer when those they care about make self-destructing mistakes, how must God feel as He looks down from the ramparts of Heaven and watches generation after generation making a botch of this thing called living.

In his great heart He must cry, "Oh, if I could somehow get inside them and make them the instant beneficiary of all that I am and have and know! I could make them a world of winners."

Two generations ago a man, fifty-six years old and broken in health, made plans to leave his invalid wife at home in England and take the message of the gospel of Christ to the Belgian Congo. When friends and critics united to ask why, he announced, "Because I want to see Jesus Christ transversing the forests of the Congo in black bodies."

Saying that, Charlie Studd said it all.

God does indeed have a plan by which He Himself can invade the skins of human beings regardless of race or color. How does He do it? What is His plan?

Author and historian H. G. Wells said, "Nineteen times the world has built a civilization and nineteen times it has fallen, and no one has questioned the quality of the foundation and material"—nobody but God, that is. God is going to build a new world with new people. The new people are the result of human nature being refined and reinforced by God's own presence in the heart.

Through their religions men have reached out in search of God. But if they could find Him by reaching out, they would have Him right where they want Him, at arms' length. God, however, will never be satisfied until He lives *within* this "temple" that our spirit, soul and body represent. God has been on the *outside* ever since Adam led the human race into sin, *wanting to get in.*

Since Adam's sin all men have been born apart from the life of God. Alive physically, they are dead, cut off spiritually. Physical, emotional and mental life abound in them. Godward there is nothing—a void. No fellowship, no love, no longing for His presence or His ways. At most an attitude of peaceful coexistence with whatever is out there, and at worst an attitude of active rebellion.

Into that void came Jesus and upset the spiritual apple cart of the most religious people in the land of Israel.

"You must be born again to get into the Kingdom of God."

"What!" cried Nicodemus. "I have to go back into my mother's womb and be born again? Impossible!"

Jesus said, "You received physical life by virtue of your physical birth, 'What is born of the flesh is flesh.' (John 3:6) Now then, to be a part of My Kingdom you must have a second birth. This time the inner you— your spirit—must be brought into contact with God. And what is born of the Holy Spirit is your own spirit."

"Nicodemus, in spite of all of your 'religion,' God must invade your personality by His Spirit or you will never enter the Kingdom of God."

There is a beautiful example of the new birth in the Old Testament. Under the direction of God, King Solomon built a twenty million dollar temple. Its value was not because of its size. In all probability the church you attend is several times larger than Solomon's temple. Rather, the value was in its contents and its workmanship.

The temple consisted of three parts: the outer court, the inner court, and the Holy Place. Upon completion of this wonder of the world, an eight-day dedication was held. One person, however, was conspicuous by His absence.

For eight days the temple contained no God. Then when the dedication reached its climax and the people were at one in praising and thanking God, the One for whom the temple was intended made His presence known. In a great and majestic cloud God descended upon the scene. Every mortal fell upon his face as God assumed residence in the Holy Place.

Now what does that 3000-year-old story teach us? That the temple was a symbol of man. You, me and all the other morally fallen six billion people who have populated planet earth. Of incalculable value and certainly awesome workmanship, we stand empty. Built to be a container of the Builder, God is most conspicuous by His absence.

Then certain Divine and human conditions are met. God comes suddenly to the temple. Man becomes a container of the living God and that is what is meant by the new birth. The hymnist said,

Surely in temples made with hands
God the most high is not dwelling.
High above earth His temple stands
All earthly temples excelling.
Yet He whom heaven cannot contain
Chose to abide on earth with men
Built in our bodies His temple.

IN SUMMARY

Questions for your discussion and study

1. What is God's plan for transforming defeated people into winners? Ezekiel 36:25-27

2. What scriptural basis did C.T. Studd have for wanting to see "Jesus Christ transversing the forests of the Congo in black bodies"? Colossians 1:27; Revelation 3:20

3. Show how "human religion" has a tendency to want to control God, while in true religion God controls and motivates man.

4. Think about ways in which the Old Testament temple is a picture of the individual believer today. 1 Corinthians

3:16, 17; 6:19, 20; Psalm 139:14; 2
Chronicles 5:11-14

Chapter 2

The New Birth: Who Needs It?

The colors in the fine oil paintings covering the walls of the living room were especially outstanding. Bright, cheery and alive, they indicated that the artist most surely was a healthy and vibrant outdoorsman, of a cheerful disposition and a positive outlook on life.

In truth, the painter was neither healthy nor an outdoorsman. I would walk across the street to visit him once a week or so. Though we became friends, he never shook my hand or met me at the door. His life depended upon a fuse. Should the fuse blow, or were there an electrical failure, the young artist's life would go out with the lights. He lived in an iron lung, a victim of polio before the introduction of the Salk vaccine.

Unable to move any part of his body but his head, he painted with a brush held between his teeth. He showed a remarkable talent though he had never painted before being stricken.

One day while sharing the Scripture with him, I was interrupted by another caller who said, "Don't tell this man he needs to be born again. He doesn't need conversion for he has never been in the 'far country.'"

The objection came from a man who had been a pastor for over fifty years, and it took me by surprise. He thought I was being extremely boorish to suggest that this fine young man might need to be born again.

His reference to the "far country" meant in substance that only those who are like the prodigal son of Luke 15 need to be born again. Since my artist friend had never wasted his father's money, drunk with the drunkards, or visited prostitutes, he patently needed no conversion, and could rest in the accomplished fact that he was baptized as a baby.

Are there, indeed, those who do not need to be born again? To answer the question let's look more closely at the parable referred to by the venerable pastor.

A gentleman farmer had sons that were a study in contrast. The older was dependable, hard-working and respectful. The younger evidenced his rebellion to all the accepted virtues by demanding his share of the inheritance early and then proceeding to waste it in immoral conduct. Finally, broken in spirit, he returned to his father asking only to be hired as a farm hand. Because of the new attitude in his boy the father welcomed him home, and threw a party in celebration.

Out in the field the older brother heard the dance band and came in to investigate. Upon seeing his younger brother royally welcomed, he was filled with anger at his father. This scoundrel-brother should not be getting such treatment! He ought to starve in the far country! His bitterness revealed he was on no better terms with their father than was his prodigal brother. They just had different ways of expressing their rebellion. One was an open sinner, the other was a secret sinner. Both were out of touch with their father. Both needed repentance, both needed conversion, both needed to be born again.

The level of our sinfulness does not determine our need of the new birth. The "moral" white collar sinner and the sin-sodden derelict equally are candidates for conversion.

God's argument with us, primarily, is that we are spiritually dead. How we behave within the confines of our spiritual graveyard is not of first importance. The fact that we are indeed dead in trespasses and sins is.

Once in a while I see a person who is so outwardly fine that I conclude he does not need to be saved. (The terms "born again," "saved", "converted," can have slightly different shades of meaning, but for our purposes shall be considered as synonymous.) But God has never met one who doesn't need it. He says plainly that there is not one righteous, not one that does good, that all have turned aside and have all become unprofitable (Romans 3:10-12).

The prophet Isaiah said all our righteousnesses are as filthy rags in God's sight (Isaiah 64:6). Now tell me, if that's what our best efforts look like to a holy God, what do our sins look like?

Two men went up to the temple to pray. One a Pharisee famous for his reli-

gion, and the other a publican famous
for his corruption. The Pharisee thanked
God that he was not a low-life like the
publican, pulled his skirts a little closer
and sanctimoniously went on his way
home. The publican couldn't even lift his
head. He knew no flowery prayers and
could spout no psalms. He knew only
that he was rotten through and through.
He hit his chest in bitter remorse for his
ways and prayed, "God be merciful to
me a sinner." I don't have to tell you
which one was forgiven.

When religionists declare that either
they or others are above being born
again, they are taking the position of the
elder brother and the Pharisee in the
temple. In their pride they reject not
only the truth of their sinfulness but
also reject God's method of salvation.

Naaman was a Syrian general with a
bad case of leprosy. Of the three varie-
ties, all were fatal. Some could be cov-
ered over better than others, but all
ended in certain death. So the general
went to Israel to see the prophet Elisha
(2 Kings 5:1-19), who instructed him to
wash seven times in the Jordan River.
Naaman was beside himself with rage.
He'd come all this distance just to wash

in the water of Jordan when he had better and cleaner rivers at home? Whoever heard of curing leprosy like that? Naaman wanted Elisha at least to perform a little magic on him. He rebelled mightily at God's method of cleansing. Yet, when he humbled himself and followed the prophet's instructions, he was instantly cured.

Today much of the religious world rebels at God's method. As a church body they see themselves as quite whole, having no need of being born again. In so concluding, they seek to establish a righteousness of their own, a religion of self-produced goodness. Now we are back to Isaiah's words that all *our righteousness* is as filthy rags. Without the Holy Spirit, self-righteousness is the best man can achieve, and it is not enough. God will never accept our righteousness to atone for our sins. I wonder why not? Why does God take such a dim view of our natural goodness? To some it might seem bigoted of Him.

Imagine yourself in the middle of the desert. You have had no water for twenty-four hours. With your last bit of strength you mount the next sand dune and your eyes feast upon an oasis—you are saved. Stumbling into the tiny settlement you make straight for the well. A well-meaning person lowers the bucket and hands you a drink from his own cup. It is then that you realize you are in a leper colony. The body of your well-meaning benefactor is ravaged with the disease. Everything that pertains to him is defiled by the germs that promote the sickness. All he owns and surrounds himself with is beyond purification. It can only be burned with fire to stop its potential for death. Now, are you going to accept the water from the leper's cup? No, you are not. Everything that the leper does is polluted by what he is. He is a leper!

The Bible says that sin in us is like leprosy. From center to circumference we are sinful and no amount of good deeds will alter that fact. Whatever we attempt to do is defiled by what we are; hence, all our righteousness is as filthy rags to God.

Jesus told the most religious man of His day that he must be born again. He told him twice so he wouldn't forget it.

Joe Stump was a good boy. Everybody said he was, and he believed it. To be an even better boy he followed his author-father into the ministry. After ten years of ministry he became depressed over the death of a close friend. While Joe stood tongue-tied, his friend went into eternity, his eyes transfixed with fear. Needing a change of scenery Pastor Stump took a train to New York City. Through a chain of circumstances, Joe ended up in the Bowery Mission. There, in the company of prostitutes and alcoholics in every stage, Joe Stump, the Rev. Joe Stump who wore spats and tails in the pulpit, was "born again."

Upon returning home he led his wife, church secretary and five hundred members of his congregation to salvation.

Who needs to be "born again"? Everybody needs it. If Nicodemus, Saul of Tarsus, and Joe Stump needed it, everybody does. Every man born once needs to be born twice. People who are born only once will die twice. Those born twice will die only once.

IN SUMMARY

Questions for your discussion and study

1. Are there those people who are so *good* that they don't need to be "born again"? Romans 3:9-23; Luke 13:3-5; Isaiah 64:6

2. What is God's first argument with us—

our level of sinfulness or the fact that we are spiritually dead? Ephesians 2:1-5

3. Think about a biblical illustration that describes how sin has invaded and polluted the total man. 2 Kings 5; Leviticus 13 and 14

4. What does the statement "Born once—die twice; born twice—die once," really mean?

Chapter 3

The New Birth: How Does It Happen?

We have seen that the new birth—being born again—is a happy reunion between God and man at which time God by His Spirit actually enters the human personality. Man becomes the dwelling place of God.

The question is, How can such a thing happen? A holy God has been offended by rebellious people. His righteousness and holiness demand that these sinning people be punished, banished from His presence forever.

Man, for his part, has been universally content to live outside of God's fellowship. He delights in his independence even to the point of flaunting it. It's obvious that there must be an adjustment on God's part and man's part before there can be a reunion.

God's sense of justice must be satisfied. The full punishment for the crimes of the human race must be exacted. How can this occur without forever destroying the people He wants to be reunited with?

Fortunately God is not only righteous, but also forgiving. This part of God's nature demands that sinful people be forgiven and restored to His fellowship. How can both sides of God's nature be satisfied?

The answer is found in the provision of a perfect substitute who will serve in the role of a willing sacrifice.

A very rowdy rural school had no success in holding teachers. One after another they left the district to the jeers of seventeen- and eighteen-year-old eighth graders. One day, though, a teacher of another sort arrived. He informed the students that it was their school and they could make the rules. And they did—no stealing, no cheating, no fighting, etc., until they had ten governing principles listed on the blackboard. Then they decided upon the punishment for breaking these rules—ten whacks across the bare back with a willow stick.

School proceeded with a great deal of

success. In three months the students learned more than they had in the previous three years. One day a lunch sack was pilfered. *Who did it? Come forward for your whipping!* After a long, long wait the littlest boy in the school came forward. He begged not to have to remove his coat. *Remove it!* When he did, it proved he had no shirt. Just a skinny, trembling, pathetic little thief. Punishment, though, must be handed out or the entire government of the school would crumble. *Get the willow stick!*

Just before it fell, the biggest lunker in the school, Big Jim, strode to the front and, pulling off his shirt, asked, "Can I take his whipping for him?" Hearing no objection from the trembling thief, the teacher exacted the full penalty of the law from the substitute, and let the offender go free.

Now that's a simple story, but it does illustrate what God did for sinning humanity. In sending His own Son, Jesus Christ, to die on a Roman cross, God's sense of justice was fully satisfied. From that day forward God has had no more reason why sin cannot be forgiven. Jesus' final words were, "It is finished." He had paid for all the sins man had committed in all the ages and the provision for salvation was now complete. God was reconciled to man. He had no further arguments against him (2 Corinthians 5:19).

But what of man? If there is to be a reunion of the alienated parties then man too must have a change of attitude. What about the sins that made it necessary for Christ to die? What about my desire for independence from God? Oh yes, my sins are bad enough in themselves, but even worse is the rebel attitude toward God that they betray. The shots fired on Fort Sumter that precipitated the Civil War didn't do much damage, but they were eloquent in declaring the rebellion of the Confederacy.

It was, therefore, not enough that Christ should die for my sin. That is, His death will not save me until I respond properly to it.

I must adopt a new attitude toward my Christ-crucifying sin. That new attitude is called repentance. Before Big Jim took the whipping for the little guy, the teacher questioned the fellow concerning his attitude toward his thievery. Inasmuch as he was truly sorry for his sin and would take Jim as his substitute, he could be forgiven and restored to schoolhouse favor *without* punishment.

What we are saying is that Christ died *for* us, in our place, and in our behalf. He was punished so that we need not be.

Because Christ died for us and we have responded properly to His death, it is now possible for Him to live in us. Sin had to be dealt with before fellowship with God could be restored. Isaiah 59:2 says, "Your iniquities have separated between you and your God, and your sins have hid his face from you." The one-two punch of Christ's atoning death and the sinners' repentance destroyed the wall of sin that had kept us from union with God. With that barrier gone God can live within us and we can know experientially the friendship that our spirits have craved. When we embrace Christ, we gain the Father's full approval.

Years ago a very wealthy man had a son. Shortly after his birth the wife and mother died. Not inclined to remarry, the rich man hired a nurse to care for the boy. A warm and loving relationship grew between the tot and his substitute mother. When the boy reached 21, he also died. Crushed by the tragedy and feeling beyond hope, the father died and in the absence of a will the estate was put up for public auction. The aging nurse attended the sale for one purpose. She wanted to buy the picture of the boy that hung in the hallway. No one else cared about the picture so she got it for a few cents. Taking it home she cleaned the glass and in the process a document fell from behind the picture. It was the missing will. In it the rich man left everything to the person who loved his son enough to buy the picture.

No illustration is perfect, but one thing is certain and that is that God wants us to love and receive His Son. To those who will, He opens His treasure.

Revelation 3:20 pictures Christ on the outside of the heart waiting to get in. "Behold, I stand at the door, and knock: if any man hear my voice, and open the door, I will come in to him, and will sup with him, and he with me."

The new birth is having our sins forgiven and receiving Christ into the heart. How do we let Him in?

It is vital to see that all of us are found on one of five levels of spiritual receptivity. This is most aptly described for us in Elmer Murdoch's book, *Step Up to Life.*

Step 1 is being "unconcerned," and so we all were at one time. We simply didn't care about sin, God, Heaven or hell. There were no eternal thoughts in our mind. Then something may have occurred to bring us to Step 2. We became "concerned." Perhaps a real scare, a death in the family, or the conversion of a close friend served to awaken us. Most of us are on Step 2. We are concerned now and want to know more.

Step 3 is being "convicted." This is the point in our lives when our sins bother us. It is the result of the Holy Spirit applying the laws of God to our conscience. Step 4 is being "repentant," that is, when our sins bother us enough to turn from them and we are prepared for Step 5, which is "faith in Christ." We are now ready to receive Him into our hearts and this in turn requires five more steps. Although not always conscious acts, these are a part of every true conversion. They are:

1. A recognition of personal sinfulness.
2. A recognition of the right of Christ to rule and control our life.
3. A full and permanent surrender to God to the extent that we understand.
4. An act of faith in receiving Christ.
5. A public confession of Jesus as Lord, and belief in our hearts that God raised Him from the dead (Romans 10:9,10).

To these acts of faith the Spirit of God gives immediate response. He applies the blood of Christ to our record of sin in Heaven. We are justified. Just-as-if-I'd never, never sinned is our standing before God. In the same moment of time He places His own life into the heart of the seeker, causing him to be born again.

IN SUMMARY

Questions for your discussion and study

1. How did God solve the problem of forgiving man, yet still satisfy His sense of justice? 1 John 1:9; Romans 3:21-26

2. What do you see to be the most important truth contained in the story of the rowdy schoolhouse?

3. What caused God to be reconciled (at peace) with man? Colossians 1:20; 2 Corinthians 5:18-21

4. What act on man's part makes him reconciled to God? Acts 3:19; Isaiah 55:6,7

5. What is the barrier that separates God

and man? Define the barrier to the best of your ability—a one word answer will not suffice! Isaiah 59:1,2

6. List the five levels of spiritual condition.

7. List the five components of every true conversion.

Chapter 4

Substitutes for Assurance

As a boy, I was loyal to religion, but disinterested in Christ. In the passage of time I became acquainted with a group of truly Christian teenagers. One facet of that relationship had a deeply troubling effect upon me. It was a little chorus that we sang. Fancying myself a singer I participated with vigor until I came to one phrase, "Do you *know* (beyond the shadow of a doubt) that you've been born again?" The answer to the musical question produced a lot of inner discord. I did not *know* that I was born again. I had religion, church loyalty, Bible knowledge, daily Bible reading, baptism, confirmation, a disgust for the grosser forms of sin, a desire to defend that which was right, but no inward assurance that I was a Christian. So sold was I on my own righteousness, I concluded I was God's child on the basis of the type of reasoning that said, "If a fine fellow like me is not a Christian, who in the world is?"

I have since discovered that I was not alone in accepting substitutes for assurance.

One day, while in this same state of mind I was challenged to pass out Christian literature at a notorious roadhouse a few miles from my home. Being assured that this was the Christian thing to do, I went. Entering the dark, smoky, smelly, bowels of that establishment I began to pass out gospel tracts to the people in the booths that surrounded the dance floor. Before long a heavy hand was laid upon my shoulder and a gruff voice said, "Don't tell me that you're twenty-one, kid. Get out!"

Now my "Christian service" endeavor had added to it the embellishment of "persecution." Fired for the task I stood outside the door and gave tracts to the folk going in and out. Soon three young men approached the door. As I handed them tracts, one of them laughed embarrassedly and said, "We know more about that than he does, don't we, John!" It was not long before "John" came back. He loomed tall as he stood before me, hands jammed in the pockets of the long topcoat that was the garb of the day. "So you're a Christian, huh?"

"Y-yes," was my reply.

"You really know that for sure, huh?"

"P-p-positively," I lied.

"Then you shouldn't be afraid to die, should you?"

"N-not even a little bit," I trembled.

"Then how about stepping into this dark alley with me," he insisted.

I never went into the dark alley. When it seemed my heart would beat right out of my chest, he broke down. "I know what you are doing is right. Me and my friends are students at a Bible college in Minneapolis. We came down here because we thought we could sin without getting caught." Leaving the others behind he got into the car and went home.

Now God had a twofold purpose that night. One was to catch those rascals in their hypocrisy and the other was to drive home to my heart the realization that I was bereft of any real assurance of being born again. I had accepted a substitute for assurance.

Actually, there are three common substitutes for assurance of salvation. They are spiritual interest, Bible knowledge and pseudo-spiritual experience.

The Bible gives us the case history of a man who was so filled with interest in matters pertaining to the Spirit that he risked his reputation and journeyed to the wrong side of the tracks for a nocturnal interview with Jesus. Captivated by the miraculous works of Jesus, risking reputation as well as the dangers involved in walking the dark streets of a great city, and religious to a fault, this man would seem surely to be born again. But he was not. He was the object of Jesus' piercing charge, "Ye must be born again." He was Nicodemus, *the* ruler of the Jews. He had spiritual interest, but no assurance of being born again.

Let's follow another long-robed man into his garden. He picks his mint, anise, and cumin. One part for God and nine parts for himself. There he is in the market, asking, "Was this egg laid the day after the Sabbath?" He could not purchase it if the hen had worked on the Sabbath to produce it. To look into his eyes is to realize that your encounter is with a deep and disciplined mind. All five books of Moses—Genesis, Exodus, Leviticus, Numbers and Deuteronomy—have been committed to memory, along with the 150 chapters of the Hebrew hymnbook, the book of Psalms. He is knowledgeable to the most intimate detail in the lives of the kings and prophets of Israel. Surely this man has assurance of a right standing with God! Wrong again. This man belongs to the sect of the Pharisees, who with others of like ilk, crucified Christ. Bible knowledge is no substitute for assurance of salvation.

Finally, let's follow the tallest man you have ever seen into a cave in the Judean mountains. In that cave, there's a woman quite accustomed to unusual spiritual experiences. Upon the tall one's request she conjures from the dead the prophet Samuel. Doesn't this kind of spiritual reality prove one's right relationship with God? Most assuredly not! For the scene depicted is that of King Saul's interview with the witch of Endor. Witches were meant to be put to death, so contrary were they to God's purposes and Spirit.

Spiritual interest, spiritual knowledge and spiritual experiences have value, but are not to be mistaken for assurance of salvation.

IN SUMMARY

Questions for your discussion and study

1. List three common substitutes for assurances of salvation.

2. Give a biblical illustration of each from reading:
    John 3
    Exodus 22:18
    Deuteronomy 18:10
    1 Samuel 28:6-25

3. Explain why each can exist apart from true conversion.

Chapter 5

New Attitudes

What are the valid proofs of being born again? Can we really know it has happened to us? One of the evidences is that we discover in ourselves a sense of newness. Paul said, "If any man be in Christ, he is a *new creature:* old things are passed away; and behold, all things are become *new*" (author's italics). The key word here is "new."

The born again person has a new attitude toward sin. Sin used to be a pleasure, but now it produces inward pain and grief. Old things (pertaining to self pleasing) have passed away. Things that once produced a temporary happiness have been revealed for what they are, empty promises of satisfaction. The born again person is still temptable and under stress of temptation sin will look attractive. But the new dimension of insight allows him to see through those things and recognize them for the shabby promises that they are. Should a person fall into the sin, his new attitude toward it is even more clearly defined. Upon sinning, the born again man finds an immediate loathing of himself and what he has done. His new nature abhors the corruption that has invaded it. He rejects it and purges it from him by renewed confession to God (1 John 1:9).

A little girl had a pet pig. She raised it with a bottle, washed, trained, and dressed it up complete with ribbon. Every chance the pig got, however, it made straight for a puddle. Seeking a satisfactory solution to its behavior, the girl went to a veterinarian who (as the story goes) transplanted a lamb's heart into the pig and the mud puddle tendency was curtailed.

It is consistent with a pig's nature to lie down in the mud. It is consistent with the lamb's nature to stay out of the mud. A pig seeks it out and enjoys it. A lamb may fall in the mud, but its first response is to get out. It is that "first response" that we are concerned about when we speak of having a new attitude toward sin. The Christian no longer *enjoys* sin. He has been forever spoiled by "new" things.

Coupled with a new attitude toward sin is a new attitude toward God. Every age has its heroes. I recall the rousing cheers from the first five rows of the old Roxie Theater as the Lone Ranger rode to the rescue around the same rock for the five hundredth time. We lived in that drama and went home to repeat it again and again. As I grew older, my heroes changed. My big brothers, athletes, and others took the place of the Lone Ranger. Included in my list of heroes was *not* God or His Son. To hear Him mentioned in any way other than a swear word was to die of embarrassment. There was definitely an inner aversion toward His company and His people. Upon being born again a new Hero arose in my heart. I found that I loved God: I enjoyed being in His presence, in the presence of spiritual people. I would walk away from a dance feeling empty, enter the kitchen where my parents were studying the Bible together and feel *wonderfully* whole. The more I experienced of His presence the more unsatisfactory were all the things that I used to be consumed with. It was not a pain to submit to Him, but a further source of inner happiness to be more obedient.

This new attitude toward God produces in us a brokenness. By that I mean that we assume a teachable attitude. Mere church members are characterized by hardness,

Christians by brokenness. Ask a church member if he has been born again and he will puff up and hiss, "Do I look like a heathen?" Ask the "born again brother" and he will respond, "Oh yes, God found me in my sin and has changed my life." Both answers are similar in that they mean yes, but one betrays hardness and the other brokenness. A broken person never defends his sin. He confesses and forsakes it instead. And a broken man never gets angry when asked if he is a Christian.

The fourth thing new in the Christian is the novel place of the rituals and symbols of Christianity. Rituals and symbols are not wrong. They have a meaningful place. What is wrong is dependence upon them. The born again man has *experienced* what the symbols stand for. Never again will he have to exchange a symbol for an experience. Baptism, confirmation, church membership, and liturgy are no longer means to gain salvation, but expressions of a living experience within. Show me a person who is hung up on the symbols and I will show you a person who has not been born again.

These four then, a new attitude toward sin, a new attitude toward God, hardness replaced by brokenness and the absence of dependence upon mere rituals and symbols, are bona-fide evidences of a new work of God within the heart. They indicate that old things have indeed passed away and all things have become new.

IN SUMMARY

Questions for your discussion and study

1. How would you describe the born-again man's new attitude toward sin?

2. What is *new* about our attitude toward God?

3. Why is brokenness an integral part of the Christian life? Psalm 34:18; 51:17; Isaiah 57:15; Isaiah 66:2

4. Why is it that it is easier for people to embrace the symbols of Christianity than the Christ of Christianity?

Chapter 6

The Harbor Master's Secret

Picture a harbor master as he seeks to steer a ship safely into harbor in the dead of night. Aiding him are three important lights. When he sees the three individually he is off course. When he steers in such a way as to see them merge into one, he is bringing the ship safely to the wharf. This is the harbor master's secret of navigation.

In determining whether or not we are born again there are three "harbor lights" that will give evidences as to the correctness of our course.

The first light is the *light of a changed life*. Our actions and our reactions begin to change. Our goals have been sublimated. Our interests have been altered. We are now concerned with those things that will last forever.

I discovered while working for a Jewish

man (who was an agnostic) that the strangest thing to him about Christians was that they tithed. The first time I made $1,000.00 in one month, he smiled as he handed it to me and asked, "You mean you are actually going to give $100.00 of that away?" I answered yes and said, "You live for time; I live for eternity. That's the biggest difference between us." He agreed, "Yes, that is correct. I never thought of it that way before, but all I care about is here and now."

The changed life is one lived in the light of eternity. Suddenly everything we do, big and small, has eternal implications. We weigh every decision and activity in the light of its eternal value. Certainly this is change, big change, for people who were formerly content with "eat, drink, and be merry" for tomorrow they might die.

The second light in the harbor is the *light of the Holy Spirit's* witness. God's Spirit stands ready to confirm His presence the instant that sin is repented of and Christ is received by faith. When we surrender our will to Christ the Holy Spirit assures us that the blood has blotted out our sins and given us a right standing with God. More on this witness of the Holy Spirit will be shared in a later chapter.

The third light in the harbor is the *light of the Word of God.* Without knowledge of the truth concerning sin, Christ, His death and resurrection, repentance and faith, it is quite impossible for us to come to experiential or even an academic knowledge of God.

The Scripture plays an important role in bringing us the assurance of being born again. It tells us what God has done, what we must do, and what God will do in our behalf when we do our part. Just how the Scriptures accomplish this will also be enlarged upon later. Suffice it at this point that a *combination* of the changed life, the Holy Spirit and the Word of God leads us to full assurance of being born again. When these three lights merge into one, we are assured of safe entrance into the harbor.

IN SUMMARY

Questions for your discussion and study

1. Read 2 Corinthians 5:17; Romans 8:16; 1 John 5:13 and learn more what the three lights stand for in this story.

2. What new concept invades the life of the born-again man that changes his life?

3. What two conditions must be met before the Holy Spirit can bear witness to the heart?

4. What truths must we be aware of before we can know God?

Chapter 7

The Seven Sneezes of Salvation

Seven Evidences of the New Birth

Seven centuries before Christ, there lived a wealthy woman in the tiny city of Shunem in Israel (2 Kings 4).

She had wealth, position and security, but she seldom smiled. She often wept for loneliness, and her aging husband was little comfort. Laughing children outside her gate only seemed to depress her and remind her of the reproach she carried. She had no child.

Sitting by her window she observed the occasional passing of the prophet Elisha and his servant, Gehazi. She asked her husband to build a special room on the wall for the prophet. To show his appreciation for the hospitality shown by the couple, Elisha sought for a way to compensate them. Gehazi astutely observed the absence of children and when this was brought to Elisha's attention, the prophet promised the couple a child within the coming year.

So a child of miracle was born, raised, and loved by the Shunamite couple. One day the young boy was on his way to the field where his father was working. He complained of a bad headache, so his father sent him home. Mom rocked and cared for him all morning, but by noon the little fellow was dead.

Without wasting a moment she sent for Elisha. When he arrived, the boy was lying coldly upon his bed. Elisha stretched himself upon the boy and prayed until the boy's body began to warm. He then began to pace back and forth, praying as he walked. He stretched himself upon the boy a second time and this time the boy sneezed seven times! Elisha returned the boy to his ecstatic mother.

The seven sneezes are significant as was the warming of the boy's body. Seven is the number of completeness in Scripture and was witness enough to Elisha that God had indeed restored the child. Moreover, the story is a picture of the new birth. Like the boy, we are stone-cold, dead before we are born again, dead in trespasses and sin. Through the gracious working of the Sprit of God we become "warm" toward spiritual truth, and finally by receiving Jesus as the Lord of our life we are restored to spiritual life.

Even as the boy sneezed seven times as an indicator of the restoration of physical life, so there are seven "sneezes" that indicate the restoration of spiritual life. One book of the Bible is particularly dedicated to giving us these evidences of being *born again*. The book is 1 John and the key verse is chapter 5:13. "These things have I written unto you that believe on the name of the Son of God; in order that ye may know that ye have eternal life." The following chapters explore the seven evidences of the new birth found in 1 John.

IN SUMMARY

Question for your discussion and study

1. How does the little boy's being "cold," then "warm," and then "alive" relate to conversion?

Chapter 8

Keeping God's Commandments

SNEEZE NO. 1: 1 John 2:3

It is inherent in all religions to *hope* for Heaven. It is inherent in Christianity to be *assured* of Heaven. Earlier we spoke of assurance coming from the consciousness of a changed life, the witness of the Holy Spirit, and the plain statements of the Word of God. John gives us at least seven specific proofs of the new birth, all of which fit under one of the above three headings.

"Sneeze" number one is 1 John 2:3: "And hereby we do know that we know him, if we keep his commandments." Evidence number one is that we have become obedient to the commandments of God. Keeping the commandments is no small problem. First, there are so many. One man counted 30,000 specific commands in the though the ten in Exodus 20 were not trouble enough! Secondly, they are very difficult for flabby-willed people like us to obey. Simply stated, some of them are really rugged.

A Christian, John says, is one who keeps the commandments. So if you say you are a Christian and don't keep the commandments, you are a liar.

The reason commandment keeping is so tough is because the laws are so contrary to our nature. They cut across our selfishness every time. Let me illustrate by quoting a commandment you probably hadn't even thought of. It is, "Give to every man that asketh of thee" (Luke 6:30). Jesus said that, and He meant it. Yet if we obey it, won't we be the object of every moocher in four counties?

A missionary was translating the book of Luke and teaching it to a group of natives who were noted for their thievery. When he got to Luke 6:30, he began to consider the implications of telling them that the God of Heaven had instructed His people to give to anyone that asks. He could see himself being wiped out. After struggling for several days, he finally translated and taught the verse. Do you know what happened? He got wiped out. They asked for and got nearly everything he possessed—money, clothes, furniture, kitchen items, all were asked for.

Through the *un*selfishness of the missionary, their own selfishness was revealed. As surely as his possessions were taken, they were returned. Due to such implicit obedience to the Word, the Spirit of God was released and the tribe was converted. Now, the Bible never says that obedience is easy to the natural, *unconverted* man. But is is possible for those who have had their natures changed. Even as disobedience is the tendency of the old nature, so obedience is the tendency of the new nature.

The multiplicity of commandments isn't a hindrance to obedience either. The marvel of all of God's laws, whether in the 10 commandments or the 30,000, is that they can be summarized by one four-letter word. That word is *love.* James 2:8 calls love the "royal law." When we truly *love,* we automatically treat God, our neighbor, our family, and ourselves right. So love is the fulfillment of the law.

I don't need to keep statistics on how well I'm doing with the other 30,000 commands. I need rather to *love* and the commandment keeping will care for itself. Romans 5:5 tells us that the love of God is shed abroad in our hearts by the Holy Spirit, which is *given* unto us at the time of the new birth.

A boy so shy that he seldom would ever speak was on his knees at the altar of a tiny church in central Minnesota. Surrounding him were a few of his friends and acquaintances. When we finished leading him in prayer (to pray extemporaneously was quite impossible for him) he stood to his feet and a smile began to spread across his face. Unprompted, he volunteered his first testimony. "I feel like doing good things to everybody. I want to help 'em instead of hurt 'em." That was it! That was the shy guy's testimony. Not eloquent, but indicative of what was happening within. The Holy Spirit was indeed shedding abroad the love of God in his heart.

When we are born again, we have a new disposition. We want to please God. We want to obey God, we want to be Christlike. This is part of the miracle that occurs when Christ becomes Lord.

One day it dawned on me. God is not trying to make everyone on earth obedient. He is working within to make us *want* to be obedient. He could easily force obedience by moving the earth a few million miles closer to the sun and raising the temperature to 180 degrees. "How do you like it?" He could ask in a thunderous voice that no one would miss. "Obey or tomorrow it will be 190 degrees."

And people would obey! At least as long as the heat was on. God is wanting something far better than that. He wants us to *want* to obey Him, so we will be obedient even when the heat is off.

God has always longed for obedience that springs from the heart. Concerning Israel He said, "Oh that there were such a *heart* in them, that they would fear me, and keep all my commandments always, that it may be well with them, and their sons forever!" (Deuteronomy 5:29).

One night I hustled home from school and began to work in the garden. When dad arrived, he watched me for a moment and asked, "What do you want the car for tonight?" He had me. I did want the car and it was the only reason I had volunteered the work. How pleased dad would have been if I could have honestly said, "Dad, I don't want anything. I just wanted to help you get the work done."

God styles Himself as a Father, our Heavenly Father. His laws were not given to cheat or frustrate us. They were given to protect, instruct, and *prove* us. When we are born again, we do by nature the things that are found written in the law. Often we fail because our minds are not perfectly instructed, but deep in our hearts we *intend* or *purpose* to do right. And God is pleased with us, in fact delighted with us, when He sees in us this heart attitude to evidence our love to Him by the keeping of His commandments.

To sum it up, we must understand that we are not born again because we keep the commandments, but rather we keep the commandments because we have been born again. This then is the first evidence of the *new birth* in the book of First John.

At this point it would be well to poll ourselves as to our attitude toward God's law. Can we say like the Psalmist, "O, how I love thy law," or are we dedicated to the pursuit of loopholes in the law?

Some who call themselves believers have in reality no "heart-affinity" toward the law of God. Inwardly they are offended by it and seek to dodge its disciplines on every hand. Those theologically trained may emphasize the fact that *grace* makes it unnecessary for us to be concerned about law. Strange that the apostle John didn't know that, when he said, "We know that we have come to know Him if we keep His commandments." No amount of mental gymnastics can escape it. It is the first sneeze of salvation, the first evidence of being born again—a brand new attitude toward the law of God.

IN SUMMARY

Questions for your discussion and study

1. The first evidence of salvation in 1 John is _____.

2. What makes commandment keeping so difficult for the natural man?

3. What is the four-letter word that enables us to fulfill the whole law? Romans 13:8

4. What is right about the statement that says, "God is not trying to make everyone on earth obedient"?

5. God longs for obedience that s_____ f_____ t_____ h_____. Deuteronomy 5:29

Chapter 9

Doing Righteousness

SNEEZE NO. 2: 1 John 2:29

The second evidence for the new birth is found in 1 John 2:29: "If you know that He is righteous, you know that every one also who practices righteousness is born of Him" (NASB). From this verse we see that the new birth makes one a doer or practitioner of righteousness.

Keeping the commandments would assure God we won't do what we *ought not* to do. And practicing righteousness would guarantee that we will do what we *ought* to do. Though the two actions are closely related, it is possible for each one to stand alone and for a person to have one without the other.

When Jesus had answered the Pharisees' pressing questions on divorce and had blessed a company of little children, a notable and rich young man of the ruling class ran to Him and cast himself at His feet.

"Teacher, what good thing shall I do that I may inherit eternal life?"

Jesus told him to keep the commandments and began to list them for the young man. Exactly where Jesus would have led him next is not determined, since the youth interrupted the Lord by saying, "All these things have I kept; what am I still lacking?"

If we are to accept his words at face value, we must conclude that he, outwardly at least, had indeed kept all the commandments. He passed the first test. We know he is not "born again" because he still senses a great lack, and asked the question.

Jesus' reply was: "If you wish to be 'complete,' go and sell your possessions and give to the poor, and you shall have treasure in heaven; and come and follow Me."

The rich young man flunked this second test. We are told, "But at these words . . . he went away grieved, for he was one who owned much property" (Mark 10:22, NASB). He was willing to keep the commandments, but unwilling to spend his life "practicing righteousness."

Practicing righteousness carries with it the idea of good works which of necessity *follows* the new birth. Of course, we are not saved by good works. But because we are saved good works follow. On this point two writers are seemingly in contradiction. Paul, quoting an Old Testament prophet, wrote, "The just shall live by faith" (Romans 1:17). Yet James said, "You see that a man is justified by works, and not by faith alone. . . . Was not Rahab the harlot justified by works? . . . Faith without works is dead" (James 2:24-26, NASB).

Are we faced with a problem here? No, only when we fail to realize that both statements can be true. By faith and faith alone we are justified before God. *But* it is by our good works we are justified before our fellow man. How else can your neighbor tell of your faith in God except by the way you act? Act as you ought to and your neighbor will justify you, saying, "Now that is a Christian!" Act as you ought not, and he will say, "That man is a Christian??"

Paul brings these two aspects of justification together in a classic passage in Ephesians 2. Here he shows us clearly the relationship between faith and works, between being justified before God and justified before men;

For by grace you have been saved *through faith;* and that [the faith] not of yourselves, it is the gift of God, not as a result of works, that no one should boast" (Ephesians 2:8, NASB, italics added).

That should settle it. Salvation comes by faith not works, and even faith is a gift. What then of James and his works? We need only to read on to verse 10, "For we are His workmanship, created in Christ Jesus *for good works,* which God prepared beforehand, that we should walk in them" (NASB, italics).

Good works do indeed follow conversion. They are the very reason for which we were brought to God. In our new walk of obedience to God, we are to begin fulfilling His plans for our life. As we *"work out* [our] salvation with fear and trembling," we are aware "it is God who is at *work in* [us], both to will and to work for His pleasure" (Philippians 2:12, 13, italics added). We work out what God has worked in. As our neighbor observes this *outworking* of the righteousness of Christ, we are justified before him.

This practicing righteousness before the world is essential because the whole world knows how a Christian ought to live. We need not resort to a holy man or even a theologian to establish what is Christian conduct. Any derelict will do. The roughest of the rough is keen to sense when a professing Christian is playing the part of a hypocrite. The derelict wants no part of living the Christ-life himself, but he well knows how you and I ought to live it.

We must show our faith by our works. If there are no works, there is not faith.

What exactly does practicing righteousness include? To answer it more than generally would fill volumes. If "practicing righteousness" is the continual pursuit of doing *right*, then perhaps we can touch on the pertinent points by an acrostic with the word "right."

R—suggests restitution. Scripture says we are to "give again that which was taken by robbery." As the born again man (with broken attitude) goes back to those he has wronged, he is indeed practicing righteousness. What a privilege it has been to see Christian growth through restitution.

John came to me one day with two four-foot-long cash register tapes in his hand. These were the items he had stolen from the local stores. Upon confession and restitution, they recorded his "purchases" on the usual tape. Do you think that the local merchants were impressed with his conversion? Do you think he felt the joy of obedience?

David was terrified of the restitution required, but he could find no lasting peace without it. Taking an older "brother" with him he made the rounds until he had a clear conscience.

During the Canadian revival of a few years ago, merchants were inundated with restitution. Ten, fifteen, and twenty year old debts were paid. This kind of Christianity made newspaper headlines.

I—stands for inhaling or input. For years the Campus Crusade people have been teaching the necessity of "spiritual breathing."

A vital part of *practicing* righteousness is the formation of a religious pattern of spiritual input. A specific time each day when the born again man is renewed within by the practice of Bible reading and personal prayer. Thus equipped and insulated by a time alone with God we can successfully cope with the pressures and temptations of an anti-Christ world.

G—stands for giving. New born Christians are notorious for their generosity. They have learned the happiness principle that it is more blessed to give than to receive. They live with a rich man mentality in spite of their poverty. So secure are they in God, so resting are they in His arms, that they are not the least concerned or worried about their future. Therefore, they give, not out of their own puny resources, but out of the vastness of the Father's resources which they see now to be their own. And this kind of giving does not impoverish them, but opens the storehouse of God to them. Show me a stingy Christian and I'll show you one who is not "practicing righteousness."

Tithing is a joy. It is the one "bill" we anticipate paying.

H—stands for helping. God so approves of this form of practicing righteousness that he gave a special gift of the Spirit to enable us to do it. The gospel needs to be believed and it needs to be preached, explained, and taught. However, until it is *demonstrated* it will have little power in changing our neighbor's life. Mow the lawn, shovel the snow, bake the cake, tend the children. Do it with a smile, with no thought of return. Do it for Jesus' sake and in Jesus' name. The kindness may be small, but the attitude that it reveals will validate your faith in your neighbor's mind.

T—stands for testimony and testimony suggests witness. Witness in turn suggests martyrdom. The same Greek word is used in both cases. To be a witness is to be a martyr. Practicing righteousness involves standing for what we believe to be right, even when it may mean the ultimate in personal loss.

Surely there is *cost* in being a disciple. The religion that costs us nothing is worth the same.

Restitution, input, giving, helping and testifying are basic to "practicing righteousness" and a beginning measure of each is to be found in the one who has been born again.

IN SUMMARY

Questions for your discussion and study

1. Give a Bible illustration of a man who was willing to keep the commandments but unwilling to "do righteousness."

2. Two writers in the New Testament are sometimes seen to be in contradiction on the importance of "works." Who are they?

3. _____ justifies us before God.

4. _____ justify us before our fellow man.

5. Give a Scripture that brings faith and works together in their proper order and balance.

6. Fill in the following acrostic to define "practicing righteousness."

R _____
I _____
G _____
H _____
T _____

Chapter 10

Overcoming Sin

SNEEZE NO. 3: 1 John 3:9

Evidence number three is found in 1 John 3:9: "No one who is born of God practices sin, because His seed abides in him; and he cannot sin, because he is born of God" (NASB).

The tendency of our life before we are born again is downward, toward evil. We are tempted to do something wrong and we succumb to that temptation.

After we are born again, the tendency of our life is upward, toward good or godliness. But let's face it, we will often be tempted to do something bad and we will occasionally succumb, as before.

However, the twice born-again person does not make *a practice* of sinning. To see this point clearly, we need to define in our minds what sin is.

Two definitions have been handed down to us by religious philosophers. The first identifies sin as any deviation from the *absolute right,* or any lack of conformity to the perfect image of God, whether we are aware of it or not. This would mean that we sin constantly, consciously or unconsciously, and would make any thought of our ever being free from sin ridiculous.

The second and better definition is that sin is *a willful* transgression of the laws of God. Accordingly, a believer, on occasion, may be beguiled by temptation and fall into sin. However, he has on such an occasion the recourse to immediately flee to Christ in confession to be cleansed and restored to fellowship with God.

The second definition of sin I see to be the only practical and scriptural approach to the problem before us. Many verses of Scripture validate this definition, while there is little to support the first. If everything short of God's perfection is sin, we will have the dubious honor of living in a perpetual state of confusion and condemnation.

God does not ask for a perfection that would necessitate our possessing *all* His attributes. He asks a perfection consistent with our realm.

A rose may be observed as a perfect rose, and it is not a perfect garden but only a perfect rose. It is not an imperfect rose because it is not the entire garden!

There is a powerful and good reason that the born-again man does not practice sinning, since "His seed abides in him"! God's Spirit has reinforced the weakness of human nature with His own strength. The Williams Translation renders the verse as "No one who is born of God makes a practice of sinning, because the God-given life principle continues to live in him, and so he cannot practice sinning, because he is born of God." God's presence is within, drawing us away from sin, convicting us, teaching us, and creating in us a strong appetite for true holiness.

A Sunday School teacher was trying to illustrate how God's strength becomes ours, or how we become strong in Christ . First, to illustrate our inner weakness, he took a toothpick and easily broke it between his fingers. Next, he bound the toothpick to a tenpenny nail and invited each of the students to try to break the toothpick. The point was made.

Our strength is the strength of a new relationship. Bound to Him, we are the recipients of His strength. This is what prompts John to further say, "And he *cannot* sin, because he is born of God" (italics added). What are the cords that so bind us to Christ that we cannot practice sin?

As a newly-married couple my wife and I set up housekeeping in a tiny parsonage in southern Nebraska. Priscilla decided to please me by making fresh biscuits, one of my mother's specialties and a favorite of mine. She had a cover over them before we sat down to dinner. With a smile and flourish she removed the cover and awaited my expression of appreciation. First, let me say, they were the wrong kind of biscuits and second they were hard as rocks. But I simply could not hurt her. I thanked her profusely and I ate heartily! Love, you will learn, will keep you from hurting your beloved.

Joseph had been sold into Egypt by jealous brothers. Only a short time there, he became keeper of all Potiphar's affairs. Potiphar trusted Joseph with the running of his entire household. One day, Potiphar's wife tried to seduce Joseph. Joseph resisted her advances and finally refused to be anywhere near her. One day as he barely slipped from her grasp, he cried, "How can I do this great sin and wickedness against my God!" In a word, he said, "I *cannot* sin."

Did he mean sex held no attraction to him? Did he mean he was physically incapable of adultery? Did he mean that God had rendered him morally incapable of such an act? Or did he mean that he loved God so much more than he loved sin that he simply could not do it?

If we forget that living the Christian life is being involved in the deepest possible kind of love affair, we will never comprehend this third evidence of the new birth. The cords that bind our weakness to the strength of Christ are cords of love. Our love for Him and our recognition of His love for us make it so that we simply cannot practice sinning.

But what does the born-again man do if he does sin? Here are three things he does *not* do. (1) He does not deny it. "If we say that we have no sin, we are deceiving ourselves, and the truth is not in us" (1 John 1:8, NASB). (2) Nor does he defend himself about it. He knows that sin is indefensible. (3) Finally, he does not excuse it. Shabby rationalizations may suffice to salve the self-centered man's conscience, but the child of God needs more than this.

What *does* the born-again man do if he

sins? He simply confesses it, with the inner determination to never grieve God in that way again. Scripture gives him plenty of grounds for this. "If we confess our sins, He is faithful and righteous to forgive us our sins and to cleanse us from all unrighteousness" (1 John 1:9, NASB). "My little children, I am writing these things to you that you may not sin. And if anyone sins, we have an Advocate with the Father, Jesus Christ the righteous," (1 John 2:1, NASB).

The born-again man is honest about his sins. As Divine Light pours into his heart he begins to see dirt in a thousand places he never detected it before, and he will be constantly resorting to the blood of Christ in order to keep his heart clean.

I was converted to Christ in a church where I was taught, "Twice-born men *never* sin." That one caught my eye! "These people must really be holy," I thought to myself. I soon found that was not exactly the case. What others, the Bible included, called "sin," the people renamed "mistakes," "infirmities," etc. This was, of course, a form of dishonesty.

Twice-born men do commit sins, but they do not practice sinning. Instead they bring to bear the blood of Christ upon their sins and find deliverance and victory.

I was away from home when my first child learned to walk. The next time I saw her was on her first birthday. My wife, Priscilla, stood her on the platform of the church and held out her hands. She tottered for a moment and then made several quick steps into her mother's arms. She tried again, and this time she fell. As her father, I was bursting with pride over her latest accomplishment. I didn't say, "Some kid! She fell down." I shouted, "Look! Look! She can *walk.*"

When we are born again, we must learn to walk. Occasionally we fall. Personally, I believe our Heavenly Father is more taken with our new steps of obedience than he is preoccupied with our tumbles. He helps us up; we learn our lesson, and we walk a more certain path for having fallen.

Do you remember how it was when you learned to ride a bicycle? First, you rode with someone else; then, with someone supporting and balancing you from behind. Finally, you were "launched" and you pedaled for all your might, all on your own. Forty years ago my oldest brother learned to ride my cousin's old "camel" bike. Since the bike was so very high he had to get started by way of the back porch. Once astride, he began pedaling down the narrow tar-paved road, and would start developing a list to one side or the other that eventually sent him into the deep ditch. Scratched and crying, he would emerge from the ditch and wheel the bike back to the porch, and get back on. Each time he progressed a little farther before hitting the ditch. He was learning to ride, but progress down the road was terribly slow due to his need to return to the starting point after each tumble.

Now, some folks have tried to live the Christian life like that. Every time they went into the ditch they thought they had to start all over again. The proper way is to pull the bike back on the road, get on right where they left off and keep pedaling. They'll soon learn to ride, to dodge big rocks and chuckholes, and to compensate for the grade. The tumbles will be fewer and farther between. That's how to make progress in living the Christ life, also.

I realize this bike story does not contain all the truth that will enable us to conquer sin. It only illustrates what happens when sin is or isn't conquered.

What, then, are the steps that the born again person takes to overcome "the sin that so easily entangles us?" (Hebrews 12:1, NASB).

Ernest O'Neill, in a pamphlet entitled "How to Stop Sinning," suggests four things. First, be clear in your own mind what sin is. Sin is conscious and willful disobedience to the will of God. When we are clear as to the nature of sin, we will be able to discern the difference between condemnation and conviction. Condemnation is what our own heart says to us when we fail to live up to our self-made standards. Conviction is the uneasy feeling given us by the Holy Spirt when we fail to live up to His standards. Condemnation is always cloudy and general; conviction is always clear and specific.

O'Neill goes on to suggest that we then deal with our guilt. Guilt can only be dealt with in one way. That is, through confession of sin. In confessing sin be honest, be specific, be penitent, and never offer excuses or share the blame with someone else. When confession is made, turn your eyes to the fact of Jesus' death. See that He suffered for the sin you should have suffered for and *receive* the cleansing that His blood provides.

The third step in overcoming is to deal with the *power* of sin. The power of sin is an unsurrendered "I" that dwells in the heart. Secretly, we feel *we have the right to behave in whatever way will be to our advantage.* It is this inner attitude that relentlessly forces us to manipulate people and God's commandments. This un-Christ-like attitude went to the cross with all the rest of our sins 2,000 years ago. This attitude died with Christ.

O'Neill states further, "Are you in despair about overcoming sin in your life? Have you come to the end of yourself? Then let the Holy Spirit reveal to you that when Christ died with all His rights, you died with all your rights. He died to His future, you died to your future. When He died to Himself as a private person, you died to yourself as a private person. . . . Now will you allow the Holy Spirit to make this real in your life?"

This dying to self-rule is what destroys the power of sin in the life.

I just finished laying 400 square yards of beautiful, cultured sod on part of my lawn. It looks great, except for the quack grass that grows even faster. After every mowing the lawn looks just fine. Twenty-four hours later the quack grass proudly raises its head. Unless I want to mow every day of my life I am going to have to find a deeper solution to the quack grass. That deeper solution is to deal with it at its roots.

Extract it—root and all from the soil. Until we deal with the power behind sin, the self, we are merely mowing off the top. When we are willing to die on the cross with Christ, we are getting to the root.

IN SUMMARY

Questions for your discussion and study

1. Give two definitions of sin that have been handed down to us by religious philosophers.

2. Why do we prefer the second? First John 3:4; James; and Romans 11 are verses that substantiate the second definition.

3. What powerful reason is there that a born again man does not practice sinning?

4. Give a biblical illustration of a man who "could not" sin.

5. What three things does the born again man *not* do about sin?

6. List O'Neill's four steps for overcoming sin.

Chapter 11

Loving the Brethren

SNEEZE NO. 4: 1 John 3:14

As the cruel Roman emperor superintended the hideous persecution of the early Church, he was impressed with a singular characteristic of the believers. Mystified, he was heard to murmer, "Behold, how they *love* one another."

With Christianity came a new kind of love. The Greeks were well acquainted with erotic and filial love. Passionate desire—sexual love—has been used and abused from the dawn of time. Love for one's own is also common. Plato wrote, "A child loves and is loved by those who begot him." The most common Greek word for love is one that can best be understood as meaning to cherish.

Yet none of the above words could adequately describe what those pagan persecutors saw in those suffering saints. It's as though it was necessary for a new word to be coined to adequately describe what was shared among the born-again crowd. The new word was *Agape,* meaning the love which is the gift of God. This love is the fourth evidence for the New Birth. "We know that we have passed out of death into life, because we love the brethren. He who does not love, abides in death" (1 John 3:14, NASB).

One of the most overused cliches is the one which says, "Birds of a feather flock together." But these hackneyed expressions have their defenses: they contain truth in a nutshell. What this one means is that there must be kindred spirits before there can be communion. There must be some common denominator that forms the bonds that draw us together. Folks gather for fellowship around a football field, a baseball diamond, a card table or a keg. These are the centers of attraction that bind them together.

For the born again, the center that draws them together is their mutual experience in Christ. The Spirit of God within has inspired love for their Father's children.

By nature we are not governed by love in our relationships to one another. We experience hatred, bitterness, injury, dislike. Even the best of friendships wear thin and we soon need to part company to preserve the "friendship." Three couples rented a houseboat to tour the islands of beautiful Lake of the Woods. In a few short days they had inter- and intra-couple feuding. Why? Because with only human love no close relationship can long endure.

How different among the "brethren." We draw love from a reservoir filled by *Another.* Of course, it was not always like that. Before we were saved we were most uncomfortable among the "saints." They were always speaking about things that made us uneasy and their very manner seemed to make us feel we were being judged. This feeling was very real and we reacted to it. Jesus called this reaction hate. He said the world hated Him and that the world would hate His disciples as well. The more Christlikeness a believer displays the more adverse reactions he will get from the world. "Beware," He warned, "when all men speak *well* of you." Again, "In this world you shall have tribulation." And, "They who live godly in Christ Jesus shall suffer persecution."

Perhaps this is why it is so vital that

Christians love one another—nobody else does and the situation is not apt to improve!

The newborn Christian has indeed found himself a family. And he loves it. Here he can be accepted, encouraged, taught, exhorted, knowing all the while that even if he is not perfect he is loved. Paul refers to this as being "accepted" in the beloved.

The all-important word describing this fellowship is the word *Koinonia*. It means a sharing of friendship and an abiding in the company of others. This loving of the brethren is such a practical thing. In Romans 15:26 it results in *practical sharing* with the less fortunate. In Philippians 1:5 it is *partnership* in the work of Christ. In Ephesians 3:9 it is *oneness with the whole believing company*.

Yes, there was a time when this weird crowd really freaked us. But upon being born again we were baptized right into the center of it and made the wonderful discovery of a love that exceeds that of blood relationships. Now we love and cultivate the company of those we studiously avoided.

Surely, there are some we love more than others, but we find that we will the highest good for all. The Christlikeness that they display seems to bank the fires of our heart and cause us to love them more. At times we must let love cover a multitude of sins in order to let brotherly love continue. But continue it does and in its continuance proves that we really are God's people. We really have passed from death into life.

Such a change has occurred in the believer that it is now impossible for him to relate to the world in the usual manner. He now differs from the world in the area of goals, priorities, and of course interests. A consciousness of eternity and of being an eternal being has invaded his person. Hence he cannot adopt any goals that do not last forever. He must give priority to things that are eternal and his interests and strong desires are going to be toward that which is lasting in the deepest sense of the word.

The unconverted man is a "time man." He refuses to think and plan beyond here and now. Death and the afterlife are subjects for immediate dismissal. A recent beer commercial reflects the view of the "time man." "You only go around once in life so you have to grab for all the gusto you can get." This is the "time man" philosophy stated or unstated. He is reaching with all his might to embrace enough of life's experiences to produce satisfaction.

Because of the great disparity in philosophy between the born-again person and the worldling, it is necessary for the Scripture to say, "Do not be bound together [unequally yoked] with unbelievers; for what partnership have righteousness and lawlessness, or what fellowship has light with darkness? Or what harmony has Christ with Belial, or what has a believer in common with an unbeliever?" 2 Corinthians 6:14.

The unequal yoke suggests a situation that demands compromise. Business partnership is a situation that would demand compromise were a believer and an unbeliever to be bound together in it. Marriage is another. Nothing but compromise and frustration can come of being unequally yoked. Why? Because the believer and the unbeliever have nothing in common. Their goals, priorities and desires are polarized.

We see, then, that the new strong attachment in love to the brethren carries with it an equal and opposite detachment from the part of the world that still clings to a Christless and eternity-less philosophy of life.

The most powerful illustration of this is a word picture painted by Paul. He said that the world had been crucified to him and he unto the world. He meant that the best that the world could offer had no more appeal to him than a three-day-old decaying corpse. Furthermore, the feeling was mutual. Paul had no appeal to a Christ-rejecting world.

In our "B.C." years we strove to gain the fellowship and approval of the world and were more than a little disgusted by what we saw in Christians, should by chance we encounter them. What a change has occurred! Since we see more clearly now we are disgusted by the emptiness of the world's offer and find ourselves drawn and bound to the fellowship of believers we once pitied.

We *know* we have passed from death unto life because we love the brethren. Our best friends are Christians; we would not even consider marrying a person who is not also a believer; in business we want the partnership of those who are of like precious faith. This love is *evidence* that we are born again.

This evidence for the new birth deals a deadly blow to prejudice on every level. Red, yellow, black, white, or polka dot— *Agape* love extends to all. Just in case someone, somewhere, would profess to know Christ and still harbor in his heart a prejudice against another race, John concluded this evidential statement by saying, "He who does not love abides in death." Notions and opinions may be altered, but unless the love of God has flooded the heart, we abide in death.

One day a man had a dream. In this dream he was taken to hell. Hell appeared to him as rows and rows of people seated at overflowing banquet tables. In spite of the abundance of food they suffered the agonies of starvation for their arms were encased in splints making it impossible to bring the food to their mouths.

Suddenly the scene changed. Now the man is in Heaven. To his surprise the situation looks much the same. A great company of people is seated at long and overflowing banquet tables. Their arms are also encased in splints. But instead of the agony of starvation there is radiance, health and satisfaction. They are feeding each other across the table!

IN SUMMARY

Questions for your discussion and study

1. What mystified the pagans of Rome about the Christians?

2. What Greek word came into usage to express this new love?

3. Why is it so vital that Christians love one another? John 15:19

4. According to 2 Corinthians 6:14-18 what must the believer beware of?

Chapter 12

Confessing the Lordship of Christ

SNEEZE NO. 5: 1 John 4:15

In an age long ago in Europe there existed a governing system called feudalism. All property was owned by the feudal lord and worked by the peasants for a meager share of the crops. In exchange, the lord offered protection to the peasants in time of danger and attack from enemies.

Picture the feudal lord in the heat of battle. The drawbridge has been lowered to receive the loyal peasants who lived in the outlying farms and villages. Bringing up the rear he observes a rascal who has flaunted his laws and refused to pay his taxes for years. After a moment's thought the lord orders the drawbridge drawn and the rebel left to fend for himself against the attacking hordes. He refuses to serve as savior to those who reject his lordship.

"Whosoever confesses that Jesus is the Son of God, God abides in him, and he in God" (1 John 4:15). A confession that Jesus is the Son of God carries with it deep meaning. It is first and foremost a confession that Jesus is indeed King of kings and Lord of lords. This confession carries with it certain moral obligations. Once we recognize Him for who He is our days of independent actions are over. Failure to bring our life under His authority is to forfeit our hope of salvation. He, too, refuses to serve as Savior to those who willfully reject His Lordship!

In his fine book on apologetics, *Know Why You Believe*, Paul Little gives four possible attitudes toward Christ's claim to divinity.

The first attitude is that He is merely a *legend* and that it was in later centuries that *other* people called Him God.

However, erroneous legends do not arise in the lifetime of a great man's contemporaries. All four Gospels which attest to Jesus' claim of divinity were written before 70 A.D. If those Gospel writers had added to Jesus' word, they would have been mobbed for being liars.

Second, then perhaps He was a *liar.* Liars abound and they also found religions. So, perhaps He said He was God in order to give weight to His teachings? If He lied, He would have disqualified Himself from being a great moral teacher and surely the prospect of death at the hands of the barbarous Romans would have brought the truth out. He was crucified because of His claims to deity. If He was a liar, just before the beating began you would have expected Him to say, "Ahh, I was just kidding about being God."

The third option is that He was a *lunatic,* a sincere, but self-deluded person who is to be compared with a man who fancies himself to be Napoleon Bonaparte. There is a place these days for people who go about thinking and saying that they are God. If His claims to be God were the result of being a lunatic, then the symptoms would have manifested in other departments of His life as well. Jesus showed no evidence of imbalance at any level or in any department. In fact, He showed His greatest composure under the greatest pressure. Through the entire, unjust trial and the agony of the cross, He maintained the highest level of balance, dignity, selflessness, and composure. The greater the pressure the more sharply defined were the evidences of His stability. So much for the lunatic theory.

The fourth possibility is that Jesus is exactly who He said He was—the very Son of God. A number of religious leaders have made claims to divinity, but had a small problem when it came to substantiating their claims. I visited a commune of the followers of Krishna Venta some years back. I asked who they thought he was, since he had recently been dynamited to death by an irate husband. The answer I got was, "The very same one who walked this earth 2,000 years ago." Well, what about a resurrection? What about the moral questions that surrounded his demise?

Father Divine reigned as God to his sincere followers for many years on our own eastern coast. He had a "heaven" replete with "angels." Once more there was nothing in his life to substantiate his verbal claims. Reputation blackened with charges of immorality, he also died without a resurrection.

Jesus, however, gave credence to His claims by the sinless life that He lived.

Pilate had to say, "I find no fault in

Him," and the centurions at the crucifixion added, "Surely this was the Son of God."

Even more eloquent than these testimonies are the words of those who knew Him best, such as Peter who said, "Him who knew no sin, was made to be sin for us." Jesus' character clearly justified His claim.

Jesus' power over natural forces evidenced His being the Creator Himself. He stilled storms, stunted the growth of trees, healed the sick, opened the eyes of a man born blind, and raised the dead. These things He did as proofs of His divinity.

Finally, Jesus predicted His death no less than five times. He also described the manner in which it would happen. The skeptic may counter that a number of people have accurately predicted their own deaths. Jesus did one thing more. He predicted His resurrection—and then did arise from the dead three days after His burial.

We need to be aware here that argumentation alone will not convince others of the divinity of Christ. Human beings do not necessarily recognize Him when they see Him. The Jews missed Him in spite of centuries of earnest expectation.

The twelve disciples were unaware, in spite of their close association with Him. Unless revelation comes from the Father, no human can grasp the truth of His divinity.

One day Jesus polled His disciples. "Who do men say that I am?"

They replied, "Oh, some say John the Baptist, some Elijah and others Jeremiah or one of the prophets."

Jesus persisted. "But who do *you* say that I am?"

All were dumb except Peter. "Thou art the Christ, the Son of the living God" (Matthew 16:16).

How did Peter know when the Jewish hierarchy had missed that truth? Peter knew because the Father had revealed it to him! God hides things from the wise and prudent and reveals things to those who have the right attitude—the childlike attitude He likes.

Jesus then said to him, "Blessed are you," Simon Barjonas, because flesh and blood did not reveal this to you, but My Father who is in Heaven. And I also say to you that you are Peter, and upon this rock I will build My church; and the gates of Hades shall not overpower it" (Matthew 16:17, NASB).

The church is built on the statement Peter made: *Thou art the Christ, the Son of the living God.* It is the very foundation of Christianity. No wonder the recognition of the divinity of Christ is one of the "sneezes of salvation" chosen by John.

God loves us so much that He will grant revelation to every childlike heart. How does one account for the dramatic change in the life of Saul of Tarsus?

His own testimony credits the change to a revelation from God about His Son, Jesus Christ. On the road to Damascus God *revealed* Christ *to Paul.* In the Arabian desert the revelation continued. Commenting on that period of Divine training, Paul later said, "It pleased God to *reveal* His Son *in* me."

Salvation, the new birth, is a revelation of Jesus Christ to the inner person.

Human reasoning alone will never bring us to the knowledge that Jesus is the Son of God. Scripture plainly declares in 1 Corinthians 1:21 that since "the world through its wisdom did not come to know God, God was well pleased through the foolishness of the message preached to save those who believe" (NASB).

Because God's ways and thoughts are so much higher than our ways and thoughts

(Isaiah 55:8,9) it is clear that something more than the reasonings of man will be necessary to bring us to a knowledge of God.

Three things are required to bring us to this knowledge. Two pertain to revelation and one to our response to God's revelation.

The first requirement is a logical presentation of the gospel which becomes the ground of faith. Though the mind of man will never reason its way to the knowledge of God, neither must the presentation of the gospel be unreasonable and defy the laws of learning. The gospel message is God's revelation to the mind of man. When it is understood, it is fixed upon his conscience. The devil cannot steal it away. Note: This degree of revelation does not *save*. It is only a revelation to the mind.

The second requirement in knowing God in an experiential way is the proper response. Having had the mind enlightened by the gospel story, man must then take the steps that the story prescribes. The first is *repentance*—that change of mind that alters our attitude toward sin and toward God. The second is *faith*, wherein we turn our natural faith toward Christ. Leaving all dependence upon personal goodness, we trust the finished work of Christ for our salvation.

At that point—the point of turning *to* Christ—we have fulfilled in us the third requirement for knowing God in an experiential way. It is now possible for the Holy Spirit to impart a deep revelation of Christ to our *spirit.*

The human spirit is the container of God's presence. It can be likened to the retina in the eye. Lined with spiritual nerve endings, it has the capacity to sense the presence of God and to interpret His likeness. Here the Holy Spirit implants the living Word, Christ. Here He shines His Divine light. Here Christ is revealed to be the Son of God *with power.* These findings are relayed to our conscious mind and our mouth begins to witness the good confession that Jesus is the Son of God.

So important is the inspired confession of Jesus' divinity that it became part of the test to discern evil spirit activity. As Satan worked to counterfeit the workings of the Holy Spirit, the apostles discerned his presence by whether or not those spirits (or doctrines) confessed that Jesus Christ came in the flesh. It is more than interesting to note that all the American cults that have arisen in the last 100 years fail this test. They do not know who Christ is.

To Mormons, He is a reincarnation of Adam. To Jehovah's Witnesses, He is a created being of the highest order. To Christian Scientists, He is a great teacher and metaphysical healer. But to none of them is He the very Son of God. Only the Holy Spirit can give this insight and prompt this confession.

Romans 10:9,10 tells us that "If you confess with your mouth Jesus as Lord, and believe in your heart that God raised Him from the dead, you shall be saved. For with the heart man believes, resulting in righteousness, and with the mouth he confesses, resulting in salvation" (NASB). This is not a confession of sin, but a confession of Christ. Shout it out! "Jesus Christ is the Lord of Glory! Jesus Christ is *my* Lord!" That confession is further proof that you are truly God's child. It is the fifth "sneeze of salvation."

In the beginning days of the Salvation Army, much of the work was done among the illiterates of London. An unlettered laborer heard the message and was soundly converted. With his wife and children he attended every meeting. Somehow he was still unsatisfied. Everyone else wore a certain colored jersey with lettering on it. He bought a jersey and had his wife sew on some attractive lettering he had seen in a store window. He was crushed when the officers laughed at his first appearance in the new jersey. On front and back the fancy lettering proclaimed that he was "Under New Management."

IN SUMMARY

Questions for your discussion and study

1. List four possible views about Christ.

2. Give one strong reason why He *cannot* be:
   a. a legend
   b. a liar
   c. a lunatic

3. What is the greatest evidence for His divinity?

4. What does it take to really know that Jesus is the Christ of God? Galatians 1:16

5. What confession is necessary before you can be saved? Romans 10:9, 10

Chapter 13

Overcoming the World

SNEEZE NO. 6: 1 John 5:4

"Is this vile world a friend to grace, to help us on to God?" the poet asked, as though he did not already know the answer. Indeed, the world system dominated by men who are in turn dominated by the Prince of Darkness is no friend to the believer. John surveying his surroundings says, "The whole world lies in the power of the evil one."

The world system has been under the power of Satan since Adam forfeited his dominion through sin. The world system will remain under the power of Satan until Jesus places one foot on the land and the other on the sea and claims back for all time the earth that He has purchased by His blood. And until then, the born-again gang will live as lights in this dark world.

So diametrically opposed is the Spirit of God to the spirit of Antichrist which pervades the world that worldliness or love of the world and Christianity are totally incompatible.

In recent years I have heard some spiritual midgets described as "worldly Christians." One mother said her son "was a believer all right, but just loved the world more than he loved Jesus." In truth there are no worldly Christians. *Carnal* Christians yes, but not worldly Christians. And certainly no one is rightfully called a Christian who loves the world more than he loves Jesus. The world hated Jesus, rejected Him, murdered Him, and has opposed every one of His purposes since. One cannot love a world like that and be a Christian. Rather, because one is a Christian he is enabled to overcome the corrupt system in which he lives and remain free from its satanically inspired defilements.

What is the proper attitude of the born-again man to the world? The Scripture makes for no confusion on the matter. "Do not love the world, nor the things in the world. If anyone loves the world, the love of the Father is not in him" (1 John 2:15, NASB).

However, before you become a dark and

gloomy doomsday sign carrier, realize what is meant by the "world." We are not called upon to hate the beauty of creation. It is the handiwork of God and the chief evidence of His existence. Nor are we to reject the people who inhabit it, for they too are His handiwork and are in His image. We are told to reject the world system which is controlled by the devil. We are to reject the values and goals of men who have not made Christ the Lord of their life. We are to compare every philosophy with the Scripture and reject those that are not compatible. When we do, we discover that the world is *filled* with things that do not owe their existence to God.

When God looks down at His beloved but fallen planet earth, what does He see? He sees the "lust of the flesh and the lust of the eyes and the boastful pride of life" in full control (1 John 2:16). What these stand for can best be explained by relating them to three forms of idolatry by which the children of Israel were continually seduced.

The "lust of the flesh" relates best to a Caananite goddess called Ashtoreth, who was the goddess of procreation. Connected with her worship was the complete expression of sensuality. Ashtoreth stands for the pursuit of, and yes, the worship of pleasure. It is obvious that the worship of Ashtoreth continues today. Transmitted to us in songs, novels, TV and movies is the Canaanite philosophy, "if it feels good, do it." Or more subtly in the overworked admonition found in so many places—"enjoy."

The "lust of the eyes" relates closest to the god, Baal. When Israel came into the Promised Land they were instructed to rid the land of all forms of heathen religion as well as the inhabitants. Unfortunately, they did an incomplete job of both, and both became "thorns in their sides."

Nearly eighty years ago a railroad agent sat in his dingy office in northern Minnesota and opined that there must be a better way to make a living. Investing a few dollars in watches, he had a quick return for his money. Next he accurately guessed that if a host of products could be displayed in a catalog and the book distributed to every home in the state, he'd have a fantastic business. Of course, he was correct! The young railroad agent became the founder of Sears-Roebuck and Company. The mail catalog business is based on the axiom that what we see we will want.

The god Baal promised the worshiper the

ability to buy all that his eyes coveted. Hence Baal relates to the phrase "the lust of the eyes."

Think with me through an encounter that may well have been repeated many times in Israel. A young farmer is harvesting grain under the midday sun. Past his property saunters the Canaanite who used to own it. "How many bushels to the acre?" inquires the Canaanite. "Oh, looks like about thirty," answers the Israelite proudly. "I used to own this land before you chased us out. I always got at least sixty." "Sixty? How did you do that?" "See that pile of rocks at the end of the field? That's where I sacrificed to Baal every year. He took care of everything."

That night the Israelite and his wife talked it over. Sixty bushels to the acre would mean a whole new life for them. A goat, cattle even, and an addition on the house for the new baby, and on and on.

Well, the farmer didn't exactly worship Baal. He did rebuild the altar. (He reasoned the stones needed to be picked up before he broke a plow.) The next time he butchered he did it on a windy day near the pile of rocks. He didn't really pray to Baal, he merely thought about him a while. Of course, he still planned on worshiping as

Joshua had commanded. Anyway, an amazing thing happened. Next year he got fifty bushels to the acre. Not what the Canaanite promised, but enough to spread the "new farming method" to a lot of his neighbors.

The inordinate desire to "possess" gripped the hearts of the ancients just as it grips hearts today. Life to the Baal worshiper is one long and arduous struggle to possess whatever the eye can behold. The struggle is justified by the notion that the acquisition of the next bauble will mean happiness. At last we will have caught up with the Joneses. Unless they go out and refinance! Then the struggle goes on again.

We seem to be slow in learning that neither pleasure (Ashtaroth) nor possessions (Baal) truly satisfy. There is a very simple answer for this that we will touch upon later.

The third Canaanite idol was an ugly brute called Moloch. One can experience only a certain amount of sensual pleasure before he is either satiated or perverted. "Things" also lose their charm for those who can have whatever they desire. What then remains is a lust for power, and this is where Moloch comes in. Sitting like an ugly Buddha with hands forming a fiery basin,

Moloch offered power, prestige, and popularity to anyone who would worship him. He would not content himself with money or a puny lamb. The price for the bestowal of his favors was the *sacrifice of a son*. You want to be president? Then stand before Moloch, calculate the arc and like a basketball player pitch your baby boy into the fire. The evil spirit that fostered the worship of Moloch would "guarantee" that the position would be yours. Many Israelite kings "caused their sons to pass through the fire" in order to solidify their political power.

Within our lifetime a multimillionaire who gained his fortune by importing Scotch whiskey during Prohibition days set his mind upon the acquisition of power. Realizing it was too late for himself he sought to achieve it through his sons. Utilizing his millions he gained his ends, but at a terrible price. Both sons were shot dead at the height of political careers—the price exacted by Moloch.

Remember that pleasure, possessions and power are not wrong in themselves. Each is a legitimate desire. It is when they become the end-all of our seeking that they become our enemies. They can never become the heart's center of life because they do not possess the ability to satisfy. The pleasure seeker forever seeks a new titillation, the possession monger has an eye for one more trinket, and the power moguls can't find a night's rest. Why cannot these pursuits satisfy? Because we were made for God and God alone deserves the place at the center of the heart.

Worldliness—love of the world—is being caught up in the spirit of the age in which we live. While the worldling pursues Ashtaroth, Baal, and Moloch the born-again man pursues his God. Further, he refuses to make anything the center of his life that is not eternal. In his desire to be a person of eternity, he lays up his treasure in the bank of Heaven content to live on the interest "the second time around."

The power of the world—the peer pressure, this pressure to conform—is not to be sneered at. It is a gutsy enough thing to be more than a match for anything less than the power of God.

The believer's faith has enabled him to tap that power and be lifted to a plane of living that is totally satisfying with all the crutches discarded. "For whatever is born of God overcomes the world; and this is the victory that has overcome the world—our faith" (1 John 5:4, NASB).

Besides the foregoing, there are four

more pitfalls that the twice-born man religiously avoids. These four help to summarize the "spirit of the age" in which we live.

That a young girl can be attacked and murdered on the sidewalks of a residential section of New York City is not surprising. But, when we are told that many heard her pleas for help and refused to act (they had only to dial the police), we are shaken. What is happening to us? We are fast adopting the *spectator mentality*. We let TV do our thinking, the Vikings our exercising, Farrah Fawcett our dieting, and the government our planning. This deadening passivity is setting us up for the Antichrist, marking us for that future time. A Christian should be a *doer*; he should be an active member of society, but not merely busily and feverishly doing things because no one else will. He should be finding God's plan for his life and then be forever doing it, doing it, doing it. Were you to ask such a one how a quick million would change his life, he would answer, "Not one bit." He is doing what he truly wants to do, and has no secret plans that would suddenly surface upon the bestowal of the cool million.

The spectator compensates for his inertia

by becoming supercritical. The spectator criticizes everything, and gets an active feeling of pseudo involvement for having spoken.

Eleven years ago I went to a minor league ball game. The players nearly outnumbered the spectators, who in turn criticized everyone on the field. Hitters, pitchers, fielders and umpires all were fair game. The next day, wanting an illustration that would show the difference between being a spectator and a participant, I went to the ball field and lined up for batting practice. The big black in front of me was powering pitch after pitch over the fence. Donning a helmet and armed with the lightest bat I could find I took my place in the batting cage. I found out later that the huge pitcher was none other than Dallas Green, who was just one year out of the majors as a reliever for the Pittsburgh Pirates.

Needless to say, I learned my lesson about the difference between being a spectator and a participant. My criticisms were quelled for a lifetime. The ball would slap into the catcher's mitt before I could budge the bat—it looked about the size of an aspirin, and was quite untouchable. Five minutes in the batting cage did more for me than twenty-five years in the stands.

If the believer is going to overcome in his world, he must trade in his spectator mentality on Spirit-inspired activity and creativity.

The second pitfall is the *urge for conformity*. No one dares to be different. People would rather be wrong than different. The nondrinker and the nonsmoker must explain their position.

Two men stand out as nonconformists in American literature. One was Ralph Waldo Emerson and the other was his stubborn sidekick, Henry David Thoreau. Of the two only Thoreau stuck to his guns. Jailed for refusing to pay his taxes which he thought unjust, he was visited by his friend Emerson.

"Henry, what are you doing in there?" Emerson asked.

"Waldo, what are you doing out there?" growled Thoreau in reply. To be a nonconformist in theory is one thing. To act it out is quite another. The born-again man was born again to be a nonconformist. Paul said, "Be not *conformed* to this world; but be ye *transformed* by the renewing of your mind" (Romans 12:2, italics added). Conformity is the result of pressure from the *outside*. Transforming is the result of pressure from the *inside* and God's Spirit provides that inside pressure to break the mold of the world.

The third pitfall for the born-again man to avoid is the *drive for security*. There is a fine line between living by faith and being irresponsible, but the believer must discern it. Jesus said, "Seek ye first the kingdom of God, and his righteousness; and all these things [pertaining to physical needs] shall be added unto you" (Matthew 6:33). We are to trust God for the provision of our physical needs. We are to make Him the *source* for all that we need. In all probability, our needs will be supplied through our job, but our job is still not our source. We could get fired, the firm could be dissolved. God wants us dependent upon Him and wants us to realize that dependence!

What about being successful in our work? By all means be successful. Be the biggest turkey raiser in four counties, but do it to God's glory, not for your own security. God wants to be your security. John Wesley gave good advice when he said, "Earn all you can, save all you can, so you can *give* all that you can." People who make the Lord their security leave a spiritual legacy. When Wesley died, his last words were, "Best of all, God is with us."

All he left behind was a suit of clothes, a silver spoon, and the Methodist church, the largest Protestant denomination in the world.

The final pitfall for the twice-born man to avoid is the current *loathing* for discipline.

Bums we've always had. They traipsed from the tracks to our door in a steady stream to get a free cup of coffee and sandwich. Then the beatniks appeared and finally the hippies. Beatnik came from the word "beatific" and their goal was to find the beauty in life apart from materialism. All three—the bums, the beatniks and the hippies—had one thing in common, a *loathing* for discipline.

As believers, we must take care that we don't translate our newfound freedom in Christ into a form of spiritual hippiedom.

What we need more of is discipline—control of the highest sort. We need discipline from every direction, from God, the Bible, our brethren, our teachers, and from *ourselves.* Christians have to quit taking the easy way out. The only way to have power is to accept discipline.

Let me describe two men. One is the most powerful man in America, the other the most insignificant. Mr. R has so little freedom that he can't take a drive with his wife. His day is so planned for him that he scarcely has a moment for himself. When asked to speak, he says only those things that others have prepared. His work is never done. He is on call every moment of every day. Poor Mr. R, I wonder who he is and what he does?

On the other hand, Mr. B moves through his day at an easy pace. He consults with no man. He travels when and where he wishes, dines with whom he pleases, and speaks his mind freely on any subject. He is beholden to no man and answers the phone for no one. Lucky, lucky Mr. B. I wonder who he is and what he does?

In case you have not already guessed, Mr. R is Ronald Reagan, the President of the United States of America. "B" stands for bum, for Mr. B is simply a bum. He who accepts no discipline also has no power. He who accepts discipline steps up his horsepower to Chief Executive level.

God wants soldiers not beachcombers. This involves the acceptance of discipline. Via discipline the believer steps up his spiritual horsepower to executive level and is granted responsibility that is a delight to his heart and God's.

So the believer overcomes the world.

Satan's offer of pleasure, prosperity and power have taken the mandatory eight count and been disqualified. The believer has learned to love people and use things instead of vice versa.

The spectator mentality, the urge for conformity, the drive for security and the loathing for discipline have been recognized as the traps they are and have been carefully avoided. God's power is transforming and the "world" has lost its charm.

Picture Noah. One day we will see things much as he saw them from the ark. Noah was chafed by 100 years of sneering, scoffing, and rejection as he built the ark, but went on preaching righteousness and rejected the spirit of the age in which he lived. Now he is vindicated. Obedience to God was worth it all. The water of the deluge only lifted him closer to the Lord he served. How did Noah overcome his world? *"By faith* Noah . . . prepared an ark for the salvation of his household." Noah overcame the world by faith—so will we.

IN SUMMARY

Questions for your discussion and study

1. What is meant by "the world," and

2. What is meant by the lust of the flesh? By the lust of the eyes? The pride of life?

3. Give a descriptive word beginning with the letter "p" to the above questions. Now name the Canaanite god that relates to each of them.

4. How would you define the "spirit of the age" in which we are living?

Chapter 14

The Inner Witness

SNEEZE NO. 7: 1 John 5:10

When the pastor called on the new African Christian to inquire concerning her progress in the Christian faith, she dropped her embroidery and ran into her bedroom. Returning to the living room she answered with a glow, "I'm just fine, Pastor, the Bible still says I'm saved." There is much to be said for her answer because the Scripture is certainly the source of our assurance.

However, we must not forget that the Scripture also speaks of a source of assurance other than itself. This is called, "the witness of the Spirit." It is connected with the Word since the Holy Spirit uses the Scripture when He addresses Himself to our minds. It is distinct from the written Word when the Holy Spirit functions in His capacity to convey His impressions directly to our human spirit. "The Spirit Himself bears witness with our spirit that we are children of God" (Romans 8:16, NASB). All such impressions are consistent with the Scripture and will never be found in contradiction. Without the inner witness of the Holy Spirit, Christianity would be only academic and philosophic. With the inner witness the Christian life is both philosophic and *experiential*.

A boat on Lake Michigan was enroute to Buffalo when a fearsome storm arose. In the grip of terror the passengers (all but one) met together to cry to God for help. The storm passed over and the ship arrived safely in Buffalo. Before the passengers disembarked the leader of the prayer meeting accosted the little lady who had chosen not to pray.

"I really didn't have time to pray," she explained. "I have two daughters, one in Buffalo and the other in Heaven. I was so taken up wondering which I would see first I didn't find time to pray!"

This little lady had something the others lacked. What was it? The *inner witness* of the Holy Spirit. When you possess the Spirit's witness, you are a person enjoying an experience with God, and you will never be at the mercy of a man armed only with an argument. "The one who believes in the Son of God has the witness in himself; the one who does not believe God has made Him a liar, because he has not believed in the witness that God has borne concerning His Son" (1 John 5:10, NASB).

Please remember that we are not pleading for a subjective experience outside the Word or apart from Christ. In fact, it is only as we look away from ourselves and to the Lord Jesus that the witness shines brightly. In other words, in order to have the desired subjective experience we must maintain the proper objective gaze. When as a sinner we turn from our rebellion and look to Christ upon the cross, the burden rolls from our heart. As the burden of sin falls away, a calm assurance that we are now God's child takes its place. This calm assurance or peace is the witness of which we speak. A newborn child can know little doctrine, and very few Scripture verses, and still have the witness of the Spirit. But he should not stay that way. He is to *grow* in grace and in the knowledge of our Lord Jesus Christ.

On the other hand, one can be freighted with knowledge of doctrine and have the Bible all but memorized and *not* have the witness of the Spirit. A classical case in point is John Wesley, to whom we referred in the opening pages. Wesley first heard of the witness of the Spirit at the bedside of his dying father. Before he died John heard him say, "The inner witness, that's the thing." But John was not to find it for many years. When he finally did, he wrote this definition. "The witness of the Holy Spirit is the sweet caress of the Spirit of God over the repentant sinner that enables him to cry 'abba' Father."

The above could be paraphrased by saying that the witness of the Spirit is the ability to look right into the face of God and say, "God, I know that you are my Father." "I know that I am Your child." The word "abba" is a term of endearment. It is like a frightened child whispering "daddy!" when taken into his father's arms.

At this point it would be well to distinguish between the assurance that God gives and mere feeling. Feelings come and go and are certainly no gauge of our relationship with God. With some, feelings are simply a thermometer which registers the temperature of their spiritual surroundings. The witness of the Spirit is much deeper than this. I believe it is possible to experience great religious upheaval *without* having the witness of the Spirit.

Within a span of a few weeks I had the opportunity to lead two young people to Christ. One was a boy about twenty and the other a girl of sixteen. The boy prayed with great brokenness and then testified with great joy and emotion. He then proceeded to cavort about the church hugging everybody within arms' reach, including the church secretary. This I see to be an appropriate response for such a reunion with God, but to say that everyone must behave like this to have assurance is going to put an awful lot of people under a cloud of condemnation, including myself.

A few weeks later I prayed with Mary following a gospel film. Mary was so shy that she could only pray the words that I gave her. She gave no evidence of peace or joy, and when I returned home I told my wife that Mary had come forward but I was afraid she had not gotten saved. Time proved, however, that the lad who jumped so high didn't walk so straight after he landed and little Mary had had a real meeting with God. God's Spirit bore witness to her spirit and imparted new life to her that enabled her to live a Christian life under very adverse circumstances. Mary walks with God today and the fellow, to the best of my knowledge, continues to wander in sin.

The witness of the Spirit is not mere emotion. It is far more than a "flash," an emotional "jag," or even a religious revelation. It is rather a permanent and pervading peace that tucks our soul into bed and gives us real inward rest. Spoken in the negative, the witness of the Spirit is not having any doubts about our relationship with God.

Without this final evidence of salvation something is still missing. One cannot say he is truly born of God without it. God's Spirit is neither deaf nor dumb. He is not an impersonal force. "Because you are sons, God has sent forth the Spirit of His Son into your hearts, crying, 'Abba! Father!' "

If this witness of the Spirit is really the crowning evidence of the new birth, why do so many deeply religious people struggle so long without it?

The most obvious answer is that the Holy Spirit, being the Spirit of truth, cannot witness to what has not happened. "Man looks at the outward appearances, but God looks at the heart." All outward conditions may seem to have been met, but God *knows* the heart. He has said that we will find Him when we search for Him with our *whole* heart (Jeremiah 29:13). Until we have, there is no salvation. Hence no witness.

Unfortunately, salvation has been reduced by some to a "plan" or "formula" as though certain religious functions would produce a relationship with God. But praying even all the right words with the proper inflection will not touch God if it is not from the heart and the expression of the whole heart. We must come to God by believing in His provision in Christ, giving our whole life to Him, and then trusting Him and Him alone to save us.

Sometimes people only want a *part* of Christ. They like the idea of His being a Savior, but still prefer to govern their own lives. They would put a new patch (Christ) on an old garment (self) and consider this to be the Christian life. That is not the Christian life, but a caricature of it. Worse than that it is a mockery.

Years ago a college student came forward to receive Christ. I used every verse I could think of and every prayer. I rebuked Satan, I encouraged him, I tried to elicit a profession of faith. Finally, I gave up and took him home to see the evangelist who had done the preaching. Ed Folden looked him straight in the eye and asked, "Do you want to give your whole life to Christ or do you just want some kind of religious experience?"

It was plain that Ed had spent all the time he was going to spend if his answer was the latter. The young man paused a long moment. He was had. He really had never intended to give his whole life to Christ. But he chose to now and the result was that a short moment later a newborn man in Christ was enjoying the witness of the Spirit.

In some cases well-meaning people have sought to duplicate a friend's spiritual experience. The result is that they have been looking in the wrong direction, hence the light cannot break through. Some equally well-meaning people have given their testimony in such a way as to encourage people to look *away* from the Savior to their own experience. Paris Reidhead tells the story of a man who was converted while hanging under a railroad bridge. He had been caught in the middle and his only option was to hang by his hands until the train passed. Trembling with terror he cried out to God and was wonderfully converted. When he told his best friend about his conversion, his friend said, "That sounds just like what I need."

Pointing in the direction of the trestle the new convert said, "Let's get going then."

God wants to meet with us on His terms and in His way. He is so aware of all of our needs that He will condescend to tailor-make a meeting with us that will be as unique as we are. We must look to Him and Him alone and not let our vision be clouded by an attempt to imitate others.

The final reason some have not the witness is that a secret sin or idol has not yet been abandoned. God sees it though no one else may be aware. An old Methodist evangelist by the name of John T. Hatfield once began to pray with a man that had been abandoned by all other counselors as hopeless. Hatfield told the man to open his mouth. When he did, Hatfield said, "I see a big red steer down there." And he was right. God had shown it to him. The man in anger had butchered his neighbor's steer because he was always getting into his garden. When he confessed his sin and made restitution for the steer, the witness of the Spirit came.

Connected with this idea of secret sin is a sense of condemnation that sometimes blurs the vision and so keeps us insensitive to the voice of the Spirit. Satan accuses and condemns and confuses. There are times when we must rebuke and bind the lying spirits of Satan before assurance will come.

Eighteen years ago I was preaching nightly in a Salvation Army corps in Duluth, Minnesota. God visited in a remarkable way. While praying with a little girl, I became aware there was something hindering her. The Spirit of God told me it was a demon of unbelief. I could scarcely believe that such a sweet little girl could be so vexed. I proceeded to bind the demon of unbelief, nonetheless, and in seconds a great peace came to her heart and was eloquently registered on her face. She went on her way with joy.

Knowing you are born again is a brand-new truth to millions of American church-goers. Yet, today there is a great awakening to this ancient biblical truth. You can know that you are born again.

• You will know it by your new attitude to the Law of God. (1 John 2:3)

• You will know it by the doing of righteousness. (1 John 2:29)

• You will know it by the victory over sin that Jesus gives. (1 John 3:9)

• You will know it because you love the brethren. (1 John 3:14)

• You will know it because Jesus Lordship has been revealed to you. (1 John 4:15)

• You will know it because you can overcome the world. (1 John 5:4)

• And you will know it because the Holy Spirit Himself has come within you, given you the assurance that God is your Father and you are His child. "The one who believes in the Son of God has the witness in himself."

IN SUMMARY

Questions for your discussion and study

1. What would Christianity be *without* the witness of the Spirit? 1 Corinthians 2:9-16

2. What must we have in order to experience the desired subjective experience?

3. What is your definition of the witness of the Spirit? Read Romans 1:16 and Galatians 4:6,7. What did you learn?

4. List several reasons why very religious persons may yet lack the witness of the Holy Spirit.

Chapter 15

Counterfeit Conversion — The Religion of Fear

"Test yourselves to see if you are in the faith; examine yourselves! Or do you not recognize this about yourselves, that Jesus Christ is in you—unless indeed you fail the test?" (2 Corinthians 13:5, NASB)

The Bible seems to recognize the existence of four kinds of men. There is the natural man who is consistent in pleasing himself regardless of the rights of all others including God. Then there is the spiritual man who has made God's happiness and the good of others his goal. Third, there is the carnal person. He is either like the newborn babe in Christ who still needs to be fed with milk, or he is a spiritual retard whose growth has been arrested by a return to selfishness. All of these are spoken of in 1 Corinthians 2:14—3:3. The natural man is outside of Christ. He has never been regenerated. The spiritual and carnal men are on different stages of growth in the Christian life.

If the above mentioned three were the entire cast in the drama of life on the late great planet earth, it would be relatively simple to judge righteous judgment. Unfortunately, the Scripture refers to yet another segment of humanity that it must contend with. The roots are still in the natural, but their Christian camouflage is so effective that this fourth segment must be dealt with individually. These are the counterfeit Christians, the spiritual phonies.

Jesus said the gate is small and the way is narrow that leads to life and few find it. Most prefer a wide gate and a broad way. That way they can be "religious" and still live as they please. A multitude of false prophets (Jesus called them wolves in sheep's clothing) have arisen to establish a wide-gate conversion and a broad-way Christian life. Jesus said that they cannot be detected by their words or works, but only by their fruits. He gives us this insight in his closing words of the Sermon on the Mount (Matthew 7:13-23). "Not everyone who says to Me, 'Lord, Lord,' will enter the kingdom of heaven; but he who does the will of My Father who is in heaven. Many will say to Me on that day, 'Lord, Lord, did we not prophesy in Your name, and in Your name cast out demons, and in Your name perform many miracles?' "

I will not attempt to explain how a person can call Jesus Lord, prophesy in His name, cast out demons and work many miracles and still be only a counterfeit Christian. It is evident that he *can*, for Jesus said of such, "I *never* knew you; depart from Me, you who *practice lawlessness.*"

It is obvious that the broad gate and the narrow gate are two approaches to Christianity. The narrow gate is proclaimed by the prophets of God and the broad gate "Christianity" is espoused by false prophets. The test is the attitude toward the Law of God. Broad-gate conversion brings forth no fruit, no Christlikeness. Its only issuance is a practicing of lawlessness. Therefore, we conclude that any teacher, doctrine, interpretation, that minimizes the necessity of being Christlike and makes it easy to sin is of the Devil. It is counterfeit Christianity.

And counterfeit Christianity is tough to detect. In a parable Jesus gave we see good seed sowed in a field. As it matures, it becomes evident that an enemy has planted also some tares. The owner said, "Don't weed them out now, wait 'til the harvest, then they can be sorted out and burned." The truth is that a tare is so much like the wheat that it can't be detected until harvest. At threshing time the wheat has its head bowed for it is full of fruit. The tare stands stiff and straight for its head holds nothing of value. These also stand for counterfeit Christians and Jesus said their end is to be burned. It is disconcerting to note that six times in the Gospel Jesus warned of a place where there will be "weeping and gnashing of teeth" and in every case those who were bound and went there were those who wore the uniform of a Christian, but were really phonies.

The camouflage worn by the counterfeit is so effective that it fools nearly everyone but God. Often the one who suffers the deepest deception is the counterfeit himself. The church is fairly ridden with "tares." The Corinthian church had its share; therefore, Paul counseled them to "test yourselves to see if you are in the faith."

The following is submitted in the hope that it will help us to discern between true

Christianity and false. Much of what follows has been the result of my digestion of Charles Finney's chapters on true and false conversion, the religion of fear, and others. These writings I recommend for a more comprehensive dealing with the subject.

To the counterfeit Christian, serving Christ is a lot like taking medicine. It is not in the least bit enjoyable, but is certain to do some good. He reads the Bible only because he should and not because he enjoys the presence of God or he senses that his soul is being fed. After his duty is done, he quickly resorts to something that *really* interests him. Praying and going to the church is an ordeal. I once attended a church where the expression on people's faces as they entered spoke loudly that they were on their way to the dentist. Their looks as they left made one conclude that that is where they had been. The true believer enjoys it all. He prays because he likes to, reads the Bible because it lifts him, and goes to church because it's fun.

God to the counterfeit Christian is the Great Policeman in the sky and he constantly fears police brutality.

He does what he *has* to do and never what he *wants* to do. He tries to keep the commandments, but he does not love the

Law of God. He is trying only to avoid the penalty for sin which he secretly prefers, but his miserable conscience will not allow. Mark Twain complained that his conscience took up more space than any organ in his body.

The true saint actually *prefers* obedience to disobedience. He has been changed in this heart. He does whatever he pleases. He sins all he wants to. He drinks all the booze and chases all the women that it pleases him to drink and to chase, which is none at all. He is truly free. He lives a life doing what he pleases confident that what now pleases him also pleases God. Yes, you can be a Christian and do what you please for God is working in you "both to will and to do His good pleasure."

Now back to the counterfeit. He is far more afraid of punishment than he is of sin. Indeed, he continues to sin because he does not hate it, but only the punishment. The only thing that keeps him from the really delectable forms of sinning is his fear of the consequences. When he goes to church, he loves to hear sermons on "The Security of the Believer," and "The Long Suffering of God." They buoy him up and bolster his hopes. Unfortunately, the security spoken of in the Bible does not apply to him for he is not "in Christ" at all. When he sins, it is no big thing to him for he is convinced he can always be forgiven anyway—even in sin that he premeditates.

My mother-in-law was associated with a fine Evangelical church that had a youth pastor who left his wife and family to take up with a new love.

The elders went to him to seek to restore him as an erring brother. "What will you do if you persist in this?" they asked.

"Take another church later on," was the reply.

"How can you do that in the light of what you have done?" they questioned in disbelief.

"First John 1:9," was his cool reply.

Such a man is a counterfeit Christian, a false prophet, and a blind leader of the blind. Such an attitude toward sin cannot exist in the heart of a true believer.

The counterfeit has a spirit of *get* instead of *give*. His favorite verse seems to be, "It is more blessed to *receive* than it is to *give*." In fact he finds it very hard to give at all. He views his possessions as his own and wants to part with *none* of them. Giving to God's Kingdom drains away the resources of his own little kingdom where he is king, prime minister, *and* chancellor of the exchequer. When he begins to pray, he reveals himself. He prays only for himself and his needs and his desires.

My wife had a class of ninth grade girls and the subject was prayer. She showed them the verse that said whatever we ask in prayer we will receive. Snippy little Wanda popped up and said, "Oh yeah, I tried for a new dress and didn't get it!" When my wife turned the class to James 1 where it says, "you ask and receive not because you ask amiss, seeking to consume it upon your own lust," Wanda retorted in a huff, "You mean I can't pray selfishly? Then what's to pray for?" Selfish little Wanda was later converted and became a very Christlike young woman who is now serving as a missionary.

The attitude of the counterfeit Christian is always and forever, "What's in it for *me*?"

Fear, selfishness, self-deception characterize the life of the counterfeit. Though in so many ways like his valid counterpart he is yet as lost as the wildest Hottentot.

The bogus believer may argue that he is *moral, prayerful, zealous,* and *conscientious,* and that may be. But Matthew 23:28 says, "Even so you too outwardly appear righteous [*moral*] . . . but inwardly you are full of hypocrisy and lawlessness" (NASB). Mark 12:40 describes people who *pray* long prayers and then devour widows' houses. Concerning *zeal*, the Pharisees traveled about on land and sea to make one proselyte and then made him two times a son of hell (Matthew 23:15). They were so *conscientious* that they tithed the smallest products of their little gardens, but overlooked justice, mercy, and faithfulness.

The counterfeit Christian has never had a change of heart. His ultimate intention is still to please himself. He is a humanist at heart and dedicated to the promotion of his own happiness. Oh yes, he wants to be religious because he thinks religion will guarantee his future. He only wants to *use* God to promote his personal interests. He has never had anything but a selfish thought in his head and he is hymn singing, verse spouting, and church working his way straight to hell.

In Milton's *Paradise Lost* the writer sees streams of people pouring into hell singing hymns. When he accosts the devil who seems to be promoting this travesty, Satan responds, "They consented to a painless operation. I severed their heads and refastened them in the opposite direction. While they march towards Hell their eyes are on Heaven."

IN SUMMARY

Questions for your discussion and study

1. What are the four types of men that the Bible recognizes? 1 Corinthians 2:14-3:7; Matthew 7:13-27

2. What is lacking in "broad-gate Christianity"?

3. What distinguishes a tare from the wheat?

4. How can we explain the miracles that proceed from un-Christlike people? Exodus 7:11; 2 Timothy 3:8

5. List several evidences of the counterfeit Christian.

6. What is the chief characteristic of the counterfeit Christian? 2 Timothy 3:2

Chapter 16
What Next?

What to Expect in the Christian Life

"And He was saying to them all, 'If anyone wishes to come after Me, let him deny himself, and take up his cross daily, and follow Me. For whoever wishes to save his life shall lose it, but whoever loses his life for My sake, he is the one who will save it.' " (Luke 9:23,24, NSAB)

Incomplete exposition of the Scriptures and unwise testimonies have often motivated self-centered people to seek Christ for selfish reasons. Glowing reports are given of peace, joy, and a place called Heaven. Though these are true, it is also true that when we seek God for His rewards rather than Himself, we do not find Him. Worse than that, fledgling Christians get a perverted idea of what to expect of the Christian life. This can result in a great amount of disillusionment. I do not suggest that we quit exalting the many benefits of being a Christian, but only that we tell the *whole* story. Jesus did. In fact, He seemed to emphasize the negatives more than the positives. He didn't seem to worry that He wouldn't have enough "takers" if He gave them the whole story. Here's how I found out what the whole story included.

Nothing but good things had happened to me and my family since we were converted. Materially we prospered. My father never owned a new car before he was a Christian. We enjoyed excellent health. I began to assume that because I was saved and filled with the Holy Spirit I was somehow "immune" to the sorrows that others experienced. Then in rapid succession, God allowed three events that shook me to my foundation. The first was the sudden death of my father, the second was a nervous breakdown that incapacitated me for the better part of a year. The third came at a time when I felt I really had it put together. I was enjoying my ministry as a pastor and I was enjoying my family. Especially little Sharon, age 5. She had been a surprise to us, but what a joy. Cute, smart, sensitive, and yes, even spiritual—we had fellowship together on almost an adult level. The summer after her fifth birthday we planned a trip to Lake Roosevelt in Northern Minnesota.

What began as a family vacation ended in a horrible nightmare. After two days at the lake we were struck by a vicious tornado that killed eleven people. Among them were my niece, my mother and little Sharon. As I looked down at the destruction from a high bank at the lakeside, my mind cried, "Is this consistent with the Christian life?" Immediately there came to my mind a passage from Job 1 that I scarcely knew. I remembered that when Job's children were all gathered in the house of his oldest son, a whirlwind came out of the east and killed them all. The answer to my question was, "Yes, it is consistent."

Just before going on vacation I had been to a Bible camp where the speaker, Jim Stone, emphasized that all God guarantees us is the comfort of His presence. He may add a great deal more, but that is all that we are guaranteed. "Lo, I am with you always." "I will never leave thee, nor forsake thee." It was at this point that God began to teach me the rest of the truth about living the Christian life.

The whole truth about the Christian life centers around what the cross means to the believer. As one who is born again, we should praise God for His blessings, His mercies, His gifts, and His goodnesses. We should expect great things from God, but in all our expectations we should not overlook opposition, obligation, and opportunity to serve. This is the way of the cross.

Opposition will be felt directly in proportion to the amount of Christlikeness that we radiate. The Jews said they loved God, but when in Christ they saw the nature of God it proved that they really hated Him. In fact, the world as a whole hated Him. It still does, and when we manifest His nature, it will hate us too. Why wouldn't the world appreciate a loving, selfless, Christlike person? Jesus said, "If you were of the world, the world would love its own; but because you are not of the world, but I chose you out of the world, therefore, the world hates you" (John 15:19, NASB).

Christlike people make unconverted people uncomfortable. Christlikeness exposes their deeds as evil. Besides, they are controlled by the devil and the devil hates saints. This leads us to another source of opposition.

Satan is in opposition to every plan of God. If God proposes good, Satan proposes evil. If God were to propose evil (hypothetically), Satan would propose good. Because of our relationship with God, Satan is against us. Because he knows his time is short and we are God's instruments for his destruction he is against us. He is panicky to defile the virgin Bride of Christ which will one day rule "his" planet.

That Satan and a sinning society is against us is no big surprise. But Jesus told it all when He warned that even our own families would oppose us. He said He came to bring a sword that would split families and that our loyalties to Him must be greater than our family ties. A multitude will rise up on judgment day to testify to the necessity of choosing Christ over family. He said that those who love father or mother more than Him were not worthy of Him.

All of this is a part of the believer's participation in the cross of Christ.

Our final opponent and the most formidable one is an enemy we have learned to know all too well. It is that yet-untransformed part of us, the "self" in us.

Watchman Nee attended a missionary conference in the Philippines where the subject under discussion was, "What is the Kingdom of God?" After listening for a considerable time the small Chinese arose and walked to the platform. Laying his hands on the heads of each of the leaders, he said in turn, "The Kingdom of God is Jesus in you." He proceeded to move through the congregation until he had laid his hands upon each and every one. By the time he finished the missionaries were thoroughly uplifted. He then returned to the platform and began again, this time saying over each one: "less the self in you." "The Kingdom of God is Jesus in you, less the self in you." There's the rub, the self in us—the habits of our life-style, our patterns of thinking, our desire to have our own way, to be the king of the hill—rise up again and again to thwart God's finest efforts in us. How we frustrate the grace of God! The only answer to self-opposition to our Christian walk is to put ourselves on the cross where we belong.

A.W. Tozer reminded us that we must make a one-way trip to the cross for His glory. Three things about a crucified person are readily apparent. First, he faces one direction. There is no looking over the shoulder for a better deal or softer alternative. He is not easily distracted, he faces one direction. Then the crucified man has no further plans of his own. The one-way trip is consummated in death, death to self-rule and planning apart from God's plan. Death is really a surrender so complete that you fall out of correspondence with your old self-centered environment. It is a complete adoption of God's plan for your life and a renunciation of your own. The crucified man has no future plans of his own.

Finally, Tozer says that the crucified man is a spectacle in good company. He is crucified with Christ. He is crucified unto the world—let the world jeer and let the spiritual softies take the easy way out. He is in good company.

You don't have to go the way of the cross, you must choose it. But if you don't choose it, you will always be dominated by self and will never know the crucified One in a very deep way. You will never know the fellowship of His sufferings.

Born-again people are born into the Kingdom with an obligation. When my tiny son was born he assumed a debt of between two and three thousand dollars. I don't refer to the hospital bill for that was *my* debt. His multi-thousand dollar obligation was simply his part of the national debt, the result of years and years of deficit spending by our leaders. The world has also plunged into "deficit spending." It is the deficit spending of sin and every child of God is born into the Kingdom with an obligation to defray it. In the Christian life we can expect obligation.

Jesus said, "If any one wishes to come after Me, let him deny himself, and take up his cross [*daily*], and follow Me" (Matthew 16:24, NASB). At the foot of your bed each morning lies a cross. Each morning you pick it up and tote it throughout the day. Each evening you commit the results of the day to God and rest up enough to pick it up again tomorrow. The flesh will complain and sometimes your best friends will divert you, but pick it up, carry it, until you have carried out all of God's plans for your life.

That may sound like bondage to some, but to the spiritually initiated it is the highest level of joy and satisfaction and you don't have to be an ascetic to enjoy it! The greatest feeling in the world is a sense of worth and there is no way to have a feeling of worth like doing God's will for your life.

The feeling of personal worth is a necessary component in the production of a "whole" person. To enjoy this feeling of worth we must be involved in a project that is commensurate with the vast potential that lies within. There is such a thing as the dignity of man. We are fearfully and wonderfully constructed. What God has endowed us with makes for our dignity.

In the days before the invention of the integrated circuit, it would have taken a building the size of the Empire State Building to house a computer that could come close to duplicating the processes of our mind. It would have taken all the energy produced by Niagara Falls to power it and all the water of the Falls to cool it. We are indeed a vast bundle of potential. Add to this the fact that we are eternal beings.

To find the feeling of worth that is necessary to wholeness, the task we throw ourselves into must be worthy of our natures. It must be as *deep* as we are, and therefore, it must be spiritual. It must last as long as we are going to last, therefore, it must be eternal.

What a waste to have mankind's greatest efforts directed toward things that only pertain to time. What a waste that a man should spend his life torturing nature to produce alcohol to deaden the potential worth of millions of others. We have an obligation to serve God and our generation in the way that will save the most souls. We live under crisis conditions. Perhaps some of the more intricate aspects of developing our talents will have to wait until "the second time around." Right now we are to focus the full force of our being on the most majestic enterprise under the sun, which is world evangelism.

Paul said, "I am a debtor," and he would not lay down his cross until he had paid his part of the debt. Failure to pick up one's cross is to fail in the Christian life. It means one has forsaken the true "fountain of living waters" for "cisterns, broken cisterns, that can hold no water" (Jeremiah 2:11,13, NASB). Jesus said His "meat" was to do the will of the Father. It means that He got His strength, His joy from daily fulfilling His obligation to God and to a lost world.

We all like days off, vacations, and the prospect of retirement (except for the aging that it suggests). In the Christian life, however, there is no discharge, no reprieve, no time when we can turn back to self-pleasing. Pick up the cross daily and carry it until Jesus comes. And have the time of your life every step of the way! No one was happier than Jesus and no man rejoiced like Paul. Cross bearing is a blast. It is never boring.

The only prune-faces the Christian life has are those who have left their cross beside their bed.

Weighing the cost of opposition and obligation the Spirit-born man sees opportunity enough in association with Christ to say, "Praise the Lord, it's worth it all!"

In 1849 a cry went across the American continent. "There's gold in them thar hills." A few men became fantastically wealthy, but most lost everything they had in their mad dash across the West. Later, gold was discovered in Alaska. Once again a few became wealthy, but actually more money was spent in mining the gold than the total worth of the gold that was mined!

The Christian has discovered a gold mine too. The opportunity before him is staggering. It is a hope of a wealth that carries with it no danger of disappointment. "Whoever believes in Him will not be disappointed.... The same Lord is ... abounding in riches for all who call upon Him" (Romans 10:11,12, NASB).

The newborn has discovered the *wealth of the Word*. He can't get enough. It feeds the inner man that he has starved so long.

The newborn has discovered the *deeply satisfying occupation* of *being a co-worker with God* in the evangelization of the world. Having ceased fishing for pleasure that the world can give, he has become an angler for the souls of men. He sees his testimony, his efforts being blessed of God and effecting change in those he loves. He weeps for joy over the salvation of his friends and family. He is ecstatic over the miracles he sees in answer to prayer. What a dimension has been added to his life! By comparison everything in the world is flat and two-dimensional. Now he has made the discovery of depth. And like a scuba diver he experiences the "rapture of the deep" as he plunges deeper into the great ocean of opportunity in being a co-worker with God.

He has discovered the *promise of the Spirit* and entered into a supernatural life. He has found the *joy of giving* and has learned to see *God's glory even in the gray times of life and is anticipating God's presence forever.*

The final thing that the new believer can expect is that God is going to deal with him so as to make him a real jewel. This means a lot of chipping, filing, and buffing for we are but a diamond in the rough to start with. He will refine us as gold and silver, says the prophet Malachi. That means he tosses us into the caldron, turns up the heat and melts us down until all the impurities rise to the surface to be skimmed off by the refiner. As the heat rises, we cry, "How long, Lord?"—until He sees His image perfectly reflected in us. But all this is painful—Very true. But God has a reason. He has chosen us and is now working in us to make such character within us that it will be consistent for God to share His reign with us forever. Amen.

IN SUMMARY

Questions for your discussion and study

1. What happens if we emphasize only the positive aspects of the Christian life?

2. What misconception can a new Christian easily fall prey to? 2 Timothy 3:12

3. Opposition in the Christian life will be directly proportional to the amount of

_____ _____ _____

_____.

4. List four principal sources of opposition. Which do you think is the most insidious?

5. What Gold Mine discoveries has the believer encountered?

Chapter 17

Testimonies That Help
(Some Don't)

I have titled this "testimonies that help" because I believe that there are a lot of testimonies that do not.

Sometimes the most dramatic testimonies are the least helpful because most of us cannot relate to the life-style that those giving them were saved from. One might even conclude erroneously that those who have not lived a life of flagrant sin need not be born again. In other cases some may tend to discredit their own testimony because it was not dramatic.

When a testimony is given that goes into great lurid details of the past life, it may well be that the devil is glorified more than the Lord.

Therefore, in selecting a series of short sentence testimonies I determined to get them from a group of very ordinary people.

Their lives will never be written up in a Sunday School paper and a book will never be written of their experiences in God. They may sit beside you in church, work in the same factory or live down the block from you. Their ordinariness does not invalidate their testimony. God has done a gracious and eternal work in their lives. Their testimony is as powerful as if they were notorious. Perhaps more so, because they can better relate to us.

In answer to the question, "How do you know that you have been born again?" a host of "God's wonderful nobodies" gave the following answers:

"I know I am saved because of God's Word. I did what it says, and standing upon the promises I am assured of salvation. There was an instantaneous change, and a realization that the burden was gone." This conversion took place in a washroom!

Another says, *"There was a new desire to read His Word. I was ignorant of it, but yet I always received something from it. My prayers were answered. I could apply the promises of Scripture to myself. Having lost the fear of God there was a sense of being justified, though I didn't even know the word was in the Bible. I found a new awareness of sin and also a sense of conflict* between good and evil and with the conflict a new power within." This from a young farm wife.

A young woman of twenty-seven says, *"I know I am born again because God's Word says that if you believe on the Lord Jesus as the one who died for us we will be saved. I believe with all my heart. My mother led me to the Lord when I was only five. I knew instantly that I was saved."*

"I no longer have the guilt feeling any more. Just the love and peace of God. It happened in an instant at a Christian Women's Club meeting," a young mother testifies.

Another says, *"I struggled within for some months . . . I knew I had to yield my all—Finally, I gave my life to Christ. I know I am saved because of the peace I have. His Spirit bears witness with my spirit."*

"How do I know? My values are changing. I go now by God's value system. The process was gradual, but convincing proof (satisfying to me) came at the first revelation."

"The birds, the clouds, everything seemed changed. I felt it right away. It has now been forty-six years since and it grows better."

"I am no longer afraid of death."

"My conscience which was haunted by knowledge of Scripture is now totally at peace."

"I have lasting peace. It has been a gradual thing for me."

"I have peace of mind and complete trust that each day will ultimately be the best and as God intended."

"The reality of the presence of God came when I got into the Word."

"Assurance was instantaneous. I offered myself to Him and it was like coming out of a fog. It was a though I had never lived before at all."

"I came to know that I had been forgiven for my sins."

"He completely took away all guilt."

"I had a sense of being forgiven and being clean. I also had a strong desire to please God."

"God has kept me from sin."

No one needs to settle for anything less than bedrock assurance of salvation. God wants us to know that we are His child. When we meet the conditions for salvation, assurance will be given by the Holy Spirit.

The exact circumstances will vary as will your personal response to what God is doing within. In fact, God will have an experience for you that is as unique as you are. *That* will be *your* testimony. Give it.

166

ABOUT THE AUTHOR

Richard Dugan is a pastor of the Highmore/Harrold parish of the United Methodist Church, Highmore, South Dakota. His ordination is with the Christian and Missionary Alliance and he has served as pastor, evangelist and Bible teacher for 27 years.

The Dugans have been married for 27 years and have five children; Sheila, Shane, Sharon (deceased), Sheri and Shawn.

Mr. Dugan has contributed articles to the Alliance Witness, Message of the Cross, Christian Life, Christian Reader, and Decision magazine.

RESPONSE PAGE

If this book has been a help to you and you would like more information on the Christian life, please fill out the following and mail to the address below.

_____Please send more information on how I can become a Christian.

_____I have just received Jesus Christ as my Savior and Lord and would like more information on how to experience the abundant Christian life.

_____Please recommend to me other literature for Christian growth.

Richard Dugan
Box 397
Highmore, S. Dak. 57345